"In today's world, everyone will have fifteen minutes of fame and spend six months as a consultant. This book does a great job of bringing a business sense to professionals in the difficult position of creating a business where they themselves are the product. It is practical, compassionate, and a good alternative to an MBA."

—Peter Block, author, *Flawless Consulting*

"Elaine Biech once again demonstrates her uncanny ability to turn the complex into reasonable simplicity. *The Business of Consulting* is Consulting 101. It covers the topic from A to Z in practical how-to milestones."

—Pam Schmidt, vice president, American Society
for Training and Development (ASTD)

"If you are thinking about quitting your job and going into consulting, be sure to read this book first! It is a practical guide to help you decide what to do and how to do it. And if you are already a full- or part-time consultant, you'll find many ideas for improving your success."

—Donald L. Kirkpatrick, past president of ASTD and
inductee into the *TRAINING Magazine* Hall of Fame

"Elaine Biech is visionary, experienced, balanced, practical, and above all, responsible. She exemplifies, in my mind, the best of what is meant by 'trusted advisor.'"

—Admiral M.P. Sullivan, assistant secretary of the Navy

"In *The Business of Consulting,* Elaine Biech has written the consummate how-to book for consultants in any field. It is a must-read for new and experienced consultants alike!"

—Barbara Pate Glacel, author, *Light Bulbs for Leaders*

"*The Business of Consulting* is guaranteed to help you focus on your most important business issues and to teach you things you'll use every day."

—Mindy Meads, senior vice president, Gymboree

"A successful consultant doesn't happen by accident—it takes lots of experience and a personal commitment to excellence. Elaine is that successful consultant."

—Joan Brown, former vice president of quality, Lands' End

"Elaine lives what she writes. I can't think of a better consultant to write a book about consulting."

—Edie West, executive director, National Skill Standards Board

"What if you could sit across the table and learn the secrets of consulting from one of the best in the field? My business partner and I did just that by meeting Elaine before we established our new business! Consider this book your meeting with Elaine."

—Suzanne Adele Schmidt, cofounder, Renewal Resources

"Biech has the uncanny ability to pinpoint quickly the key trouble spots in any organization. Her book can help you pinpoint the trouble spots in your own consulting business."

—Michael Casey, director of quality, Ryder Integrated Logistics

"Thinking of starting your own consulting business? This book will give you the roadmap and wisdom you'll need as you step out. Benefit from the guidance of a pro who's 'been there, done that.'"

—Jean Lamkin, corporate training director, Landmark Communications

"If you need innovative, easy-to-understand tips, this is the trainer's and consultant's 'bible' that delivers. Full of practical, ready-to-use ideas, *The Business of Consulting* is a great tool to add to your professional tool bag."

—L.A. Burke, director of quality, 14th Coast Guard District

Consulting colleagues

"Thank goodness for our profession that Elaine made the time to reflect on her years of consulting experience!"

—Michele Wyman, owner/consultant, Effectiveness by Design

"I wish I had owned this book when I started my consulting practice. Elaine has all the answers it took me years to learn!"

—Kristin Arnold, president, Quality Process Consultants

"*The Business of Consulting* is chock-full of practical tips that the beginning and experienced consultant will find essential. The accompanying disk is a valuable aspect of the book."

—Jeanne Engle, Goals Beyond Zero

"Elaine has that rare ability to translate her ideas into easy-to-understand writing. Buy and read her book if you want to develop a dynamite consulting career."

—Karen S. Ostrov, psychologist, owner, KONECT

"An incredible mentor, Elaine is intelligent, articulate, and full of great ideas for marketing your business."

—Marla Maeder, Maeder Design

"I treasure every opportunity to learn from Elaine Biech. She is a teaching pro. *The Business of Consulting* offers wisdom that can only contribute to your success as a consultant."

—Garland Skinner, retired U.S. Navy Captain

The Business of Consulting

THE BASICS AND BEYOND

elaine biech

Foreword by Richard Y. Chang

Jossey-Bass
Pfeiffer

San Francisco

Library of Congress Cataloging-in-Publication Data

Biech, Elaine.
    The business of consulting : the basics and beyond / Elaine Biech.
      p.   cm.
    ISBN 0-7879-4021-6
    1. Consulting firms—Management. 2. Business consultants.
  I. Title.
  HD69.C6B534   1998
  001'.068—dc21   98-7265

Quote in Chapter One from Charles Stein reprinted courtesy of *The Boston Globe*.

Printed in the United States of America.

Published by

350 Sansome Street, 5th Floor
San Francisco, California 94104-1342
(415) 433-1740; Fax (415) 433-0499
(800) 274-4434; Fax (800) 569-0443

Visit our website at: www.pfeiffer.com

Acquiring Editor: Matthew Holt
Director of Development: Kathleen Dolan Davies
Developmental Editor: Susan Rachmeler
Copyeditor: Rebecca Taff

Senior Production Editor: Dawn Kilgore
Manufacturing Supervisor: Becky Carreño
Interior Design: Claudia Smelser
Cover Design: Laurie Anderson

Printing 10 9 8 7 6 5 4

 This book is printed on acid-free, recycled stock that meets or exceeds the minimum GPO and EPA requirements for recycled paper.

For Shane and Thad,

my first two

consulting

projects

CONTENTS

LIST OF EXHIBITS

FOREWORD

Consulting, as a profession and an industry, has traditionally been viewed from many different perspectives. As a result, external consultants receive a wide variety of reactions from individuals and organizations enlisting their support and expertise. They may be welcomed, rejected, praised, blamed, challenged, or simply tolerated. The list could go on and on.

Shortly after I left the corporate world and started my own consulting firm, a number of colleagues and acquaintances asked me questions, such as "So you're in transition . . . how long until you get a 'real' job again?" or "Aren't you a little young to start a consulting firm when there's so much competition out there?" Or they made comments, such as "Wow, that's really exciting! Now you'll have flexibility and can take vacations more often." For those of you who have had an opportunity to be a consultant at some point in your career, these types of questions and comments probably come as no big surprise.

It is critical that anyone considering a career in consulting remember that there will be many different roles to fulfill. Two in particular are clearly and specifically addressed throughout *The Business of Consulting*. The first is the role of the consultant in sourcing, servicing, and retaining clients. The second is the entrepreneurial role of running a business or contributing to a consulting firm.

Clearly, these are not the only roles fulfilled by successful external consultants. However, unless these two roles are carried out with a relatively high degree of capability and passion, all of the technical subject-matter expertise of your particular consulting focus (for example, management, engineering, design, training, or financial) may never be leveraged to full capacity as an external consultant. In fact, you may not be an external consultant for very long.

I've had the pleasure of knowing Elaine Biech for over ten years. During this time, I have collaborated with her on a number of committees and on the Board of Directors of the American Society for Training and Development (ASTD). Besides seeing her in action first-hand as part of these efforts, I also had the benefit of exchanging "war stories" and "lessons learned" with her.

In fact, Elaine has always been one of the colleagues and friends on whom I could depend to share a valuable insight or practical tip that had immediate application. I knew her ideas would work because she role modeled everything she shared.

The Business of Consulting is not about the *theory* of consulting. Each chapter is filled with practical information that is invaluable for any external consultant. Much of Elaine's success as a consultant can be attributed to her ability to apply all of the principles, tools, and tips contained within this book successfully.

The first three chapters focus on some of the fundamentals of consulting. You'll find examples and information to help you reflect on the consulting landscape, including personal and organizational perspectives about consulting, some consultant myths and realities, ways to assess your personal consultant traits and skills, and how to determine what and how to charge for your expertise.

Chapters Four through Six explore some of the fundamental considerations of running a consulting business. In these three chapters, you'll find information to help you start and stay in the consulting business, including how to develop a business plan, partner with the right people, market and promote yourself, contract, and manage the financial side.

Sourcing, servicing, and retaining clients is what it's all about. However, all clients are not created equal, and all potential clients are not necessarily the right fit for you. Chapter Seven provides a wealth of helpful hints and tools for strengthening client relationships.

Chapters Eight through Ten will help you refine and mature your consulting practice. You'll find specific strategies for growing and diversifying your business, ethical considerations for running your business, and ways to fine-tune your professionalism. Some of the minor details presented in these three chapters can have major impact on your image and reputation as a consultant—two critical aspects for obtaining business.

So, after you've read through the first ten chapters, the key question is "Do you still want to be a consultant?" Chapter Eleven helps you answer this important question. If your answer is "yes," begin applying some or all of the practical tips and tools highlighted throughout the book. If your answer is "no," refer this book to a friend, family member, and/or colleague who is considering a career in consulting.

The consulting industry will continue to evolve. However, the two consultant roles described earlier: (1) sourcing, servicing, and retaining clients and (2) running a firm or contributing to running a firm, will never go away. *The Business of Consulting* will help you build greater confidence and capability for fulfilling these two vital roles.

Like many other things in life, developing a successful career in consulting is a journey. Elaine has provided a practical and useful "road map" for navigating this journey. The major strength of this book is that it is written at an implementation, rather than a theoretical level. I encourage you to draw on any or all of the practical information in this book as you further your career in consulting. Her success is proof that it works.

August 1998

Richard Y. Chang, CEO
Richard Chang Associates, Inc.

Winter 1987

Dear Peter,

For the last year I have been working harder but making less money. I have searched the library for a book, an article—anything that will provide me with a benchmark against which to compare my business. I want to know what the average consulting firm spends on marketing. How can I determine how much my employees should be billing? What is considered a good profit margin in "the business of consulting"? I will call you next week to find out whether you can recommend a book.

Thank you.

Elaine

Peter Block read my note. When I called him, he said, "I'm going to do much more than recommend a book. I want you to pull all your records together, such as your expenses for this year, your taxes from last year, your income summaries for the past three years, and your projected cash flow and income for the next year. After you have everything together, call me back. Plan to talk to me for two hours! And by the way, there isn't a book to read about this stuff!"

I couldn't believe my ears! Peter Block was going to consult with me on my consulting business! We had a great conversation. He provided me with sound business advice—you might say it was "flawless consulting"!

Peter's advice encouraged me to examine marketing dollars wisely, study business numbers and data carefully, and explore the advantages and disadvantages of hiring employees and forming partnerships. This book covers the same topics and is written in the same spirit—sound advice and practical suggestions for "the business of consulting."

For example, Chapter Five, ". . . And Staying in Business," provides 113 marketing ideas to ensure that you spend your marketing dollars wisely.

Chapter Six, "The Cost of Doing Business," describes forms and processes that I use to ensure that all the data I need for making decisions is always at my fingertips.

And Chapter Eight, "Growing Pains," will help you weigh the advantages and disadvantages of hiring employees, creating a partnership, and other forms of growing your business.

Peter's mentoring helped me make better business decisions for my consulting company, ebb associates inc. Being a successful consultant (like Peter) means that you not only provide excellent advice for your clients' businesses, but you also implement excellent advice for your own business.

The Business of Consulting has been written for several kinds of people: The individual who is considering a consulting profession and wonders how to start; the new consultant who may have mastered consulting and now realizes that there is also a business to run; and the experienced consultant continuing a lifelong learning journey who is looking for a few practical tips.

Consulting is a most rewarding career. You are no doubt a very fine consultant, but being good at consulting is not enough to keep you profitable. You also must manage your business.

This book focuses on the business side of consulting: How to develop a business plan, how to market your business, how to charge for your services, how to build a client relationship, how to grow the business, how to ensure your continued professional growth, and, of course, how to make money in the profession. To assist you, all of the forms presented in the book have been put on a disk. Pop the disk in your computer, personalize the forms with your name, and print them out to project cash flow, plan marketing campaigns, track your time, or identify your aptitude for starting a business.

My goal in writing this book was to provide as many practical tools and sound ideas as possible. Most were learned through trial and error. Perhaps this book will prevent you from making some of the same errors.

The Business of Consulting is written in the first person—singular and plural. Although I've authored the book, the employees of ebb associates inc have played a big part in shaping the content and it isn't right to use "I" when "we" did it.

ACKNOWLEDGMENTS

The Business of Consulting was authored by many wise and wonderful people. Thank you to everyone who "wrote" this book:

- Kathleen Dolan Davies, my editor, for helping me stay on schedule when I needed it most.
- Matt Holt, editor and friend, for trusting me and being almost as excited about my project as I was.
- Larry Alexander, my publisher, for providing me with so many worthy opportunities.
- Michele Wyman, my friend, for reading the manuscript and providing professional suggestions.
- Susan Rachmeler, my editor, for trying to add sophistication to my writing, prodding my prepositions into place, cutting contrary commas, reducing redundancy, and selecting precisely the right words.
- Beth Drake, my assistant, for keeping the world out and the business running while I wrote.
- Mentors—all of you—for believing in me always: Peggy Bouchard, Joan Brown, L. A. Burke, Vicki Chvala, Jeanne Engle, Linda Growney, Gail Hammack, Shirley Krsinich, Jean Lamkin, Mindy Meads, Rita Reuss, Judye Talbot, Michele Wyman, and my grandparents, who told me I could do anything I wanted to do.
- My sister Lorraine for always being available when I need her.
- Clients for allowing me to practice *The Business of Consulting* with you.
- And especially to Peter Block, for responding to a plea for help in 1987 with "flawless consulting."

August 1998

elaine biech
ebb associates inc
Portage, Wisconsin

The Business of Consulting

What Are You Getting Yourself Into?

"A person who never made a mistake never tried anything new."

Albert Einstein

Have you ever admired consultants who zip into a company, capture everyone's attention, accomplish in days what you've been struggling with for months, and waltz out with a big check?

Ever thought you might like to be a part of that glamorous profession? This book will help you determine whether you have what it takes to be a consultant, as well as whether the consulting profession offers what you desire as an individual.

WHAT IS CONSULTING?

Consulting is one of the fastest growing businesses of the decade. In *The Global Management Consulting Marketplace: Key Data Forecasts and Trends* (1997), Kennedy Information, the leading source on management consulting, predicts that management consulting will grow an average of 16.1 percent globally per year through the year 2000. Whether companies need help downsizing, installing a new computer system, building an executive team, or breaking into the Chinese market, they can call a consultant to assist with the effort. The organization requesting the assistance is usually called the "client." The term can refer to the entire organization or to the person who actually made the call.

Consulting is the process by which an individual or a firm assists a client to achieve a stated outcome. The assistance can come in the form of information, recommendations, or actual hands-on work. A consultant is a specialist within a professional area who completes the work necessary to achieve the client's desired outcome.

Consulting is not a descriptor that identifies a profession in itself. Unlike doctors or accountants, highly skilled consultants come from very different backgrounds. A qualifying adjective is required to identify the form of service or the area of expertise, for example, management consultant, engineering consultant, or performance consultant. Although consulting is not a "profession" by definition, it is often referred to as "the consulting profession." For the sake of convention, I will refer to the "profession" in this book.

The actual work of a consultant can vary quite a bit, depending on the area of expertise offered. Every consultant must be a subject-matter expert in some area—management development, organization development, training, or any profession, such as computers, security, writing, marketing, or a thousand others.

Even after you determine an area of expertise, you will want to select the actual work method. For example, if you decide to focus on the training field, you could develop and deliver your own material or subcontract material development to another person while you deliver it. You could develop material for others or you could deliver others' materials. You could even be certified to deliver others' courses, especially for the large training supplier firms.

Finally, if you are a generalist, such as a management consultant, you will need to determine whether you will focus on a specific industry.

FOUR WAYS TO GET STARTED

Taking risks. Embracing ambiguity. Practicing flexibility. Balancing both process and people issues. Managing multiple responsibilities. Tolerating extensive travel. Communicating effectively. Learning continually. Proving your worth again and again. Does this describe you? If you responded with a resounding "Yes!," consulting may be an ideal career move for you.

If you decide consulting is right for you, what opportunities exist? Think about your ultimate goal. Do you want to be a partner in one of the "Big Six"? Will you eventually own your own firm? Do you think you will always want to consult as an individual? Do you want to teach part-time at a small university and consult on the side? There are at least four ways you could enter the field:

1. *As an employee.* Numerous employment opportunities exist for you. You could join a large national consulting firm. The demand for consultants has led to a fierce competition for talent. According to Kennedy Information (1997), M.B.A.s from top schools can expect to be offered a base salary over $90,000 as new consultants with such a firm. Joining a large firm will give you instant name recognition. You could also join a small firm. Although your salary would be only half what it could be with one of the Big Six, you would have less pressure, more opportunity for a variety of projects, and more involvement in the entire consulting process.

2. *As a subcontractor.* Rather than becoming an employee, you could subcontract with a firm. Many businesses and consulting firms are looking for subcontractors who will fill in the gaps left as a result of downsizing or launching new initiatives. As a subcontractor you may have a less secure position, but you will have flexibility while gaining rich experience and developing a sense of the market.

3. *Part-time.* If you're not ready to take the plunge, you could consult part-time while keeping your present job. Some people use their vacation time and weekends to conduct small projects—with their employers' approval, of course. Consulting is natural part-time work for college and university professors.

4. *Self-employed.* You could also start your own consulting practice. This book addresses this last opportunity.

WHY CONSULTING NOW?

Consulting is one of the fastest growing professional areas in the economy. Why? Why now?

Turbulent times have increased the number of times that consultants are used to help organizations make their way through the processes of implementing technology, going global, improving processes, and negotiating mergers. The consulting projects have increased in dollar amount and duration. It is not uncommon for large-scale projects to cost more than $50 million over a five-year period. As

Charles Stein (1994) of the *Boston Globe* states, "Once upon a time, consultants were like dinner guests: They came for a brief visit, gave advice and went home. Now they are like guests who come for dinner, move into the spare bedroom, and stay for a year or two."

Trends

Two trends in the business world have brought tremendous implications for consulting. First is the trend toward outsourcing more and more services. Corporations will continue to hire more temporary professionals to assist when needed, as opposed to adding highly paid, permanent staff. Consultants temporarily provide the "people power" to complete the work at the time it needs to be completed.

The second trend is that rapid changes occurring in the world make it almost impossible for the executive team to remain knowledgeable about their industry, remain focused on their customers, stay ahead of their competition, and know instantly what to do when these factors collide in a negative way. Consultants offer the knowledge, information, data, and systems to solve the puzzle. They fill in the blanks. When the task is complete, they are on their way.

That's the demand side. What about the supply side? The same organizations that are cutting permanent staff to keep payroll down are providing a steady supply of people who need jobs and find that they can do consulting. In fact, many people cut from their jobs today may be placed in the same company as temporary employees.

Why this shuffling of the same bodies? Consultants are often more cost-effective for the organization, which can hire the skill it needs on an as-needed basis rather than train and educate staff for skills that may not be used again. Consultants can usually complete projects faster as well.

Client Perspective

Clients need consultants for a variety of reasons. Several are listed here:

- *Lack of Expertise.* The skills necessary for the growing and changing needs of an organization are not available inside the organization. Therefore organizations turn to consultants to complete projects or solve problems.
- *Lack of Time.* Even when the skills are available in the organization, staff members may not have the time to complete special projects or research.

A consultant can be a part of the organization just long enough to complete what needs to be done.

- *Lack of Experience.* Certain professions are experiencing a shortage of trained employees. Consultants can fill in until demand is met by training or hiring new employees.

- *Staffing Flexibility.* Consultants can be brought in for the short term to complete a project. When the work is completed, the organization can terminate the relationship easily and quickly.

- *Objective Outside Opinions.* Consultants usually provide fresh perspectives. Outsiders can look at a problem in a new, unbiased way.

- *New Ideas.* Consultants bring with them ideas from other firms and industries. This cross-pollination is a sure-fire way to tap into many resources. Staff members may be too close to the problem to see a new solution.

- *Speed and Efficiency.* Hiring a consultant who has experienced the same type of project in the past may be faster and more cost-effective than bringing staff members up to speed.

- *Assessment.* A consultant can provide an objective assessment, define the problem, and make recommendations.

- *Resolution.* In the case of a merger or other change of organizational structure, an outside consultant can act as an independent mediator to resolve differences.

- *Compliance.* An organization may not have enough time and may lack the expertise to comply with legal expectations. Hiring a consultant shows that an effort is being made to correct the problem.

Consultant Perspective

I frequently speak at conferences on the topic of becoming a consultant. The title I have used is "So You Want To Be a Consultant." I always ask: Why do you want to be a consultant? The responses I receive are many and varied. Perhaps you'll relate to several of the following:

- *Own Boss.* I want to be my own boss. It has always been a dream of mine. I will no longer need to take orders from anyone else.

- *No Set Schedule.* I want to be free from daily routine. I am bored with corporate life. I've worked all my life. I've been a good employee. Perhaps it's just this mid-life thing, but I feel financially secure and I want more than just a paycheck. I want something outside of the routine.

- *Greater Opportunities.* I see more opportunities now than ever. There seems to be a growing need in every company. I see consultants in our company every week.

- *Do My Own "Thing."* I have skills that I believe others will pay me for. I have a lot of experience and expertise and I'd like to set my own agenda, rather than follow someone else's.

- *Technology.* Technology has made it easier to create a fully operating office quickly.

- *Easy Start-Up.* I think it's a business that I can afford to start. I already have a computer and I can work out of my home office. The relatively low cost start-up makes it possible for me to own a business. Most other businesses I checked into required nearly $100,000 to open.

- *Freedom.* I want to work in my pajamas if I choose. This is as good a reason as any. Besides, there is a new prestige in working out of your home. At one time the consultant working from home was seen as less than professional. This is no longer true.

- *More Money.* Consultants appear to make big bucks and I want to get in on it. I'm working for a company that does not have a retirement plan. I sat down with the numbers and I believe I can spend my last ten years in the work force doing something I like and putting money away for my retirement.

- *Out of Work.* I don't have a choice; I was downsized out of a job. Actually I'm beginning to think I'm lucky. I don't think I would have made the move on my own. I think I can make just as good a living as a consultant.

- *Greater Good.* I want to make a difference. I'm not even concerned that I might not make the salary I am presently making. There is something greater calling me. I want to make a difference in the world and work with nonprofit organizations that will appreciate what I bring.

- *Security.* Corporate America isn't safe anymore. I want financial security, and I can think of no better way to ensure that than to take matters into my own hands.

- *Creativity.* I want to have the opportunity to be creative. I've always wanted to try something new, but in my job I am frequently told that it can't be done. I want to find out for myself.
- *Travel.* This may be a frivolous reason, but I want to travel. I know it may get old after awhile, but I'll deal with that when the time comes.
- *Challenge.* I need a greater challenge, but it isn't going to occur where I am now. There is virtually no room for promotions, and I could be doing the same thing for the next six years with very little professional or personal growth.
- *Self-Preservation.* I need to look out for myself. I'm in an industry that is fraught with mergers and acquisitions. I need to take care of myself and what I want out of life.
- *Location.* I want to live where I choose. The way I look at it, as long as I'm near an airport, I will be able to reach my clients.

Why did I join the ranks of the independent consultants almost twenty years ago? I have always said that it was because I am a lousy employee. I do not like to be told what to do; I like to march to the toot of my own saxophone; I like to take risks; I want to work during the hours I choose, not on someone else's time clock; I want to express my creativity; and I prefer to control my own destiny.

What about you? Have you explored why you are considering a move into the consulting profession?

MYTHS ABOUT CONSULTING

Some of the common myths you may hold about the field and the realities connected with them are listed next.

Myth 1: "Consultants charge over $1,000 per day; therefore, you will become rich consulting." Let's take a realistic look at this myth. It may seem like a huge sum of money for a day's work, but let's examine what that $1,000 covers. Let's imagine that you are the consultant. If you work an eight-hour day, you would make $125 per hour. However, as a consultant you are now an entrepreneur and it is more than likely that you are putting in a twelve-hour day. That brings your hourly rate down to $83.

Of course it's not possible to bill for 365 days per year. Take out weekends. Remove holidays and a two-week vacation (remember, there's no *paid* vacation). We can conservatively reduce your hourly rate by 8 percent. That brings it down to $76 per hour. Still not bad.

As a consultant you will not be able to consult five days every week. You will need to use one day for preparation, one day for marketing, and one day to take care of administrative jobs such as taxes, billing, research, and professional development. So now one day's billing covers four days of your time. That's 25 percent of $76 an hour or $19 per hour.

Murphy's Law states that all your clients will select the same two days in September for their off-site meetings and the rest of the month you will catch up on reading your *Training and Development* and *Harvard Business Review.* This won't happen just once each year. It may happen several times. In addition, you can bet on December as a notorious down time because of the holidays. No one wants you then. I've often wondered what really happens that month. Does no one work? Do employees turn into elves? When you add December to another bad month, you can expect to turn down 25 percent of all work because your clients' desired dates do not match your available dates. So deduct another 25 percent from the hourly fee. You are now down to $14 per hour.

You must cover all your own taxes. There is no employer to share the burden. As a consultant, quarters will take on a whole new meaning. You will not think in terms of the football score, but the check you must write to pay your quarterly taxes. In rough numbers let's say that you will pay 33 percent in various taxes. That leaves you with just a bit over $9 per hour.

You are on your own, so you must pay for your own benefits, such as health and life insurance and retirement. A very conservative estimate for this is $1.50 per hour. In addition you will have business expenses—copying costs, telephone calls, stationery, postage. These expenses will accumulate fast! It may be $2 for every billable hour. Now what does that leave you?

Looks like you're down to $5.50 per hour. Oh, and you wanted to purchase a laptop computer? On $5.50 per hour?!? That job at McDonald's is looking mighty good right now!

Actually it's not that bad. Although the realities of consulting are exaggerated in the example, you will need to be fully aware of everything that goes into a consulting fee. A daily fee at $1,000 or more sounds great. Yet when you consider expenses and non-billable hours, a large chunk of that $1,000 disappears quickly.

External consultants may make a six-figure income. Then again some consultants have trouble making any income. Some consultants make less than $50,000 a year doing the same thing as others who gross over $300,000. Statistics that identify the average consultant salaries vary considerably from source to source. It appears that, more than any other profession, consulting embodies the spirit of entrepreneurship. Free enterprise is alive and well! The potential is there. It depends on what you want out of it. It depends on how hard you want to work.

Myth 2: "External consulting means you will be able to avoid all the politics and paperwork that drive you crazy in your present internal job." The politics at your present job can keep you from being productive and effective. Perhaps politics is a game you have seen your boss play. As an external consultant, you may be able to escape the politics of your present organization, but get ready to be involved in the politics of not one but ten or seventeen or thirty-three organizations, depending on the number of clients you have. As a consultant, you will have many bosses rather than just one. You will need to be acutely aware of their needs and shortfalls, and you may need to make some difficult decisions to ensure that you remain on the job.

The big difference is that instead of dealing with the same politics all week long, you will be able to go home at night knowing that you will have a fresh set to work around or through (depending on your project) later in the week.

No paperwork? You will most likely have *more* paperwork. Not only will you have more, but unless you are starting out with an administrative assistant, you will not have anyone to whom you may delegate some of the work. Some of your paperwork will have a higher degree of importance. As an employee, you may have been able to turn your expense report in late and then beg the bookkeeping department to slip it into the stack anyway. But if you file your quarterly taxes late, the IRS is not likely to slip it into the on-time stack.

You must track hours and work so that you know what to charge clients. You must bill your clients in a timely manner to avoid cash-flow problems. You must determine how you will track invoices to ensure that your clients are paying you. You must track all expenses to avoid paying a larger share of income taxes than you should. You must track and file all paperwork so that you can locate it for your attorney and accountant and banker when they request information.

Not only will you not be able to avoid politics and paperwork, but it will be multiplied as you open your consulting business. If you don't take care of your paperwork, you will be out of business faster than you got in it.

Myth 3: "You will be seen as an expert in your area." You are probably seen as an expert in the job you now hold. People turn to you for answers; you are respected by your colleagues and praised by your bosses (some of them anyway!). Enjoy that while you can. You will be required to build that reputation with every new client relationship. You are about to face a never-ending task of proving yourself.

Starting your business goes far beyond opening an office and listing yourself in the yellow pages. You will build your business one client at a time. You will build your expertise one project at a time.

---

*You will build your business
one client at a time.*

Myth 4: "Having your own consulting practice means more free time." If you are looking forward to getting up at noon and being out on the golf course several times each week, you are in for a big disappointment. Being a consultant means that you will become a business owner—an entrepreneur. Like most entrepreneurs, you will spend sixty to eighty hours each week that first year getting your business up and running. You will be marketing your services and networking with everyone you know.

You will be working for others, most likely business people who go to work early, have tight deadlines, and experience huge pressures. You will be there to work as a partner with them to meet the deadlines and to relieve some of their pressures. You may need to work nights and weekends to meet a client's critical deadline. All the while you may be wondering when you are going to find the time to complete the marketing you must do to ensure that, after this project is completed, you will have another one waiting for you.

Myth 5: "Consulting is a respected profession." I thought I had chosen a respected profession. I was shocked the first time I was called a "beltway bandit"— the term assigned to consulting firms in and around the Washington, D.C., beltway. Since then, I've been called a pest because I followed up too often with a client. I've also been called a con man, which really bothered me even if the client couldn't tell he had the wrong gender! Jokes about consultants abound.

Some of the negativity is deserved. There are many charlatans in our business. Unfortunately, the profession lacks legal standards or legitimate certification. It is very easy to go into the consulting business. Go to your local printer and have a business card printed. You are magically transformed into a consultant before the ink is dry.

Often people who are temporarily out of work drift into consulting to pick up a few bucks. They are in the field long enough to make a mess and devalue the role of the consultant. One out of every twenty projects I accept requires me to build the reputation of the consulting profession in one of two ways: I may need to clean up a mess created by a wanna-be consultant who lacked organization development knowledge or I may find myself fighting a battle of trust due to poor ethics or overcharging by a consultant who worked with the client organization previously.

Myth 6: "It's easy to break into the consulting field. All you need to do is print some business cards." This is actually true. It is easy to break in. Staying in the business is what's hard. You did want to make a living, too, didn't you?

Initially you will need to spend at least 50 percent of your time marketing your services. You will need to establish business systems, set up your computers and printers to do all the things you want them to do, create tracking systems for money, clients, paper flow, projects, and a dozen other things identified throughout this book. You may feel exhausted and we haven't even mentioned providing services to your clients.

Myth 7: "Deciding to grow your practice is an easy decision. Everyone wants to grow a business." You would think the business of consulting would become easier. Unfortunately it does not. If you are good you will have more work than you can handle. At some point you will question whether to grow your business and how to do it. Should you produce products? Take on a partner? Create a firm? Or stay solo?

This is not an easy decision. It requires risk and capital. The pressure will be on you to grow. You must remember that there are many ways to grow without adding people to your payroll.

The responses to these myths were not meant to disillusion you. They were meant to ensure that you had both sides of the story. So let's explore what *is* great about consulting next.

REWARDS AND REALITIES OF CONSULTING

I've listed some of the rewards and realities of consulting in the paragraphs to follow. Take them to heart as you make your decision about starting your own consulting business.

Rewards

Consulting can be one of the most rewarding, yet challenging careers. Imagine sitting at a desk looking out at the scene you have chosen. Imagine waking up every day knowing that you are going to do what you have chosen to do that day. Imagine not fighting rush-hour traffic. Imagine being able to select the projects you want. Imagine working with the people you want to work with. Imagine doing what you are best at and what you enjoy most. Imagine challenging yourself and living up to your potential. Imagine being paid well to do what you love. Imagine working your own hours. Imagine feeling the satisfaction of being a part of a project that you believed in. Imagine completing projects successfully and being genuinely appreciated. Imagine being able to make a difference. Imagine working in locations that you have selected. Imagine taking the day off without asking permission. Imagine getting up in the morning and not going to work . . . but going to play! These are the rewards of consulting.

Realities: First-Year Lessons Learned

What's the first year like? Three new consultants offer you some of their thoughts about the realities of the field. Perhaps their first years' lessons will remind you of things you need to do.

Consultant Number 1. My first year was a real surprise. I had been on the purchasing end of consulting for so many years as the director of training that I was sure I knew all there was to know. So when our company offered an early retirement package, I took it. The consultants I worked with were top-notch. They made the job look so easy! I laugh now about all that I didn't know. For example, I never thought about how consultants completed all they had to do! Giving up my weekends those first months was a real shock! And I had no idea about how business was generated. I didn't know I'd have to sell! It certainly was good that the company provided a generous severance package. I used all of it and a portion of my savings to get started. Otherwise I would have starved!

Consultant Number 2. Starving wasn't my problem! I gained ten pounds my first six months as a consultant! I had no idea working out of my home would be so difficult. There were so many distractions—the lawn needed mowing, the laundry needed folding, the walk needed sweeping, the dishes needed washing, the floor needed scrubbing, the garage needed cleaning. And the refrigerator was the worst distraction! I seemed to open it every time I passed it. I had to work hard at time management and separating my business from my home. I had to make a few investments I didn't think of initially. I needed more filing cabinets and bookshelves than I thought. I had to purchase a different phone the first week—one with a mute button to silence the dog when I couldn't. I had to establish a way to track who I called, what they said, and when I needed to call them again. Fifty-three pink telephone slips floating all around the office was not a model of organization! Now I share an office area with two other people. We share the cost of a copy machine and a part-time typist and receptionist. I need the social interaction that this arrangement gives me. I need to work away from my home. I just feel more professional.

Consultant Number 3. I wish I had contacted my accountant before I started my business. I just didn't think of it. I knew I was in trouble on April 3rd when he asked me how much I had paid in quarterly taxes. In fact, I wish I had taken at least six months to plan for my transition. I took a one-year lease on an office space that I rarely used. I thought I needed to be in the middle of things to be in business. My work focus has changed from what I thought it would be. I thought I would be regularly dispensing advice to CEOs. Instead, I find myself doing more and more writing. I have the wrong software, but every time I think about installing something better, I realize that none of the files will transfer. I know that if I continue to do the kind of work I am doing, I will need to make the change. The longer I wait, the worse it gets! I just don't have the time to do it now.

What lessons are in store for you as you enter the world of the consultant?

JUST WHAT ARE YOU GETTING YOURSELF INTO?

As you can see, there are many pros and cons in the consulting field. It can be confusing. Just as you would with any major decision, you will want to conduct your own research. You will want to discover whether consulting is a profession you want to pursue.

One of the best ways to do that is to talk to other consultants. Explore your concerns and confirm your hopes by interviewing people in the profession. Most of us enjoy talking shop, especially if we work alone. As professionals we owe it to those entering the field to share our knowledge and insight. But what should you ask someone who has been in the business? Exhibit 1.1 provides a list of questions you can use to interview consultants. Also spend time thinking about the various aspects explored in this chapter and develop your own questions. How will a change affect your career path? How will it affect your personal life? Take your time in making a decision. Do your homework.

🖫 Exhibit 1.1. A Dozen Questions to Ask a Consultant.

1. How long have you been a consultant?
2. How did you start?
3. Why did you decide to become a consultant?
4. How would you describe your consulting practice?
5. How have you structured your business, and what are the advantages and drawbacks of that structure?
6. What do you do for clients?
7. What is a typical project like?
8. What is a typical day like?
9. What marketing activities do you conduct?
10. What is the greatest challenge for you as a consultant?
11. What would you miss the most if you quit consulting?
12. What should I have asked that I did not?

Exhibit 1.2 challenges you with several aspects of becoming an external consultant. Read the statements, checking all with which you agree.

Although the number of checks on the page is not significant, your willingness to face the reality of what it takes is *very* significant. Each time you are unable or unwilling to check a box, you show how closely you match the profession.

💾 Exhibit 1.2. Are You a Match for the Profession?

Quick Quiz

❑ I am willing to work sixty to eighty hours a week to achieve success.

❑ I love risk; I thrive on risk.

❑ I have a thick skin; being called a pest, "beltway bandit," or con man does not bother me.

❑ I am good at understanding and interpreting the big picture.

❑ I pay attention to details.

❑ I am an excellent communicator.

❑ I am a good writer.

❑ I like to sell myself.

❑ I can balance logic with intuition and the big picture with details.

❑ I know my limitations.

❑ I can say "no" easily.

❑ I am compulsively self-disciplined.

❑ I am comfortable speaking with people in all disciplines and at all levels of an organization.

Next rate yourself on the following points:

• *Are you willing to work sixty to eighty hours each week to achieve success?* You are about to enter the world of the entrepreneur. Perhaps you will be able to decrease the number of hours after your business is up and running, but until then it will be demanding. Most successful entrepreneurs require less than eight hours of sleep a night. Time is always a critical element to entrepreneurs. In his book,

Entrepreneurs Are Made, Not Born, Lloyd E. Shefsky (1994) teaches readers how to learn to get by with less sleep! You will eventually become more disciplined about your use of time, learn to juggle many things at once, and identify priorities.

• *Do you love risk and thrive on it?* As a consultant you will live with constant uncertainty. The biggest risk is wondering about finding enough steady work to pay the mortgage. Even if you land a year-long project with an organization, the person who brought you in may not be there as long as you are. The possibility of a change in management through a promotion, transfer, or layoff could put the project, and thus your contract, in jeopardy.

• *Do you have a thick skin?* Does being called a pest, beltway bandit, or con man bother you? Consultants are not always respected. How will you react the first time your profession or your personality is criticized?

• *Are you good at understanding and interpreting the big picture?* Clients will often hire you because they believe that you will have a unique advantage and be able to see the organization from a different perspective. You will constantly need to think outside the parameters that your client explains. You will often need to be a quick study in how the organization works, and you will need to be adept at asking the critical questions that will result in the insight your client needs.

---

*Be a quick study in how
an organization works.*

• *Do you pay attention to details?* Although you must see the big picture for your client, you will also be running a business that will require you to focus on the details of accounting, proofreading, and scheduling, among others.

• *Are you an excellent communicator?* This is critical. I cannot think of a single consultant who does not need to be a superior communicator. If you did not check this box, I would seriously recommend that you obtain additional training and development in communication before you attempt a consulting profession. It is basic and it's required. You must be able to communicate clearly and completely. You must be a good listener.

• *Are you a good writer?* Writing is almost as important as communicating. You will write reports, marketing materials, letters, proposals, and client materials. In many cases your work will go before top management. If your writing is not as good as it should be, you may want to hire someone to proofread your work or even complete the writing for you.

- *Do you like to sell yourself?* Knowing how to impress a client with your skills and abilities without bragging is an art form. It is often a matter of your attitude. You must believe in yourself and be able to convince a client that you can achieve what your client wants you to achieve.

- *Can you balance logic and intuition, big picture, and details?* A consultant must be able to put on whatever hat is required to do the job. You may be buried in the details and logic of your cash-flow projections when a client calls and asks you to brainstorm the needs of the community in 2005. Your marketing plan will be a balance of logic and intuition. You must be flexible. You must be able to tap into all of your skills and attributes.

- *Do you know your limitations?* Only you know what they are. Are they physical? Social? Financial? Might they prevent you from doing what needs to be done? We all have limitations. It's how we manage them that counts. One of my limitations is an inability to make small talk. I overcome that by planning ahead for situations in which I will be expected to make small talk. If you don't know what your limitations are, ask someone who knows you well.

- *Can you say "no" easily?* You will need to say no to some projects because they aren't right for you. (More about that in Chapter Five.) You must also stay focused on your strategy. It may be tempting to accept a project that's not right for you—especially if you don't have anything on the horizon. You also must be realistic about the amount of work you can take on. Initially it will be better to overestimate the time a project will take than to have quality suffer because you spread yourself too thin.

- *Are you compulsively self-disciplined?* You must be a self-starter. You must be compulsive about your financial records. You must be compulsive about planning and developing materials for your clients. You must be compulsive about billing your clients.

Be compulsive about
billing your clients.

- *Are you comfortable speaking with people in all disciplines and at all levels of an organization?* Depending on the project you have accepted, you may find yourself talking to crane operators, secretaries, supervisors, janitors, teachers, presidents, welders, or cooks. You must feel comfortable with them so that they feel comfortable with you.

How are you doing? Ready to learn more about the skills of a consultant?

Talents and Tolerance

"Whether you believe you can or you can't,
you will prove yourself correct."

Henry Ford

The most important reason to become a consultant is because you want to. Whereas Chapter One focused on what it takes to *become* a consultant, this chapter focuses on the skills and the personal stamina you will need to *remain* a consultant. It forces you to explore both sides of working out of your home and potential barriers to your success.

The most important reason to become
a consultant is because you want to.

You may be surprised to think of yourself as an entrepreneur, but you must examine this aspect of becoming a consultant. Your professional skills, abilities, knowledge, and experience provide the content. Your entrepreneurial abilities will determine how well you run your business. Both are required to be a successful consultant.

SKILLS FOR SUCCESS

As a consultant, you will possess skills that are valued and needed by clients who are willing to pay you for them. Naturally, many of the skills required will be dependent on the niche you will carve out for yourself. Whether you work in the manufacturing or insurance industry, whether you focus on training or organization development, you will want to acquire the skills necessary to put you at the high end of the knowledge curve.

As a training consultant, for example, you may become certified by one of the larger training supplier companies such as DDI, Forum, or Zenger-Miller. In this case you will need strong delivery skills. A training consultant who also designs training must have design skills. If you expect to broaden your consulting to working with clients on performance issues, you will need to add analytical, measurement, and process improvement skills to your list.

In addition to these specific skills, there are general consulting skills that show that you are a professional. Exhibit 2.1 provides a self-evaluation to determine whether your skills and characteristics are a match for the profession. Complete it by jotting comments in either the "strength" column or the "needs improvement/attention" column. Then read the following sections to determine which of the listed skills are important for you.

Prospecting and Marketing. Prospecting, or looking for clients, will require much of your time when you first start. Having clients is the only thing that will keep you in business. Prospecting and marketing will ensure that the phone keeps ringing.

---

*Having clients is the only thing
that will keep you in business.*

Promoting and Selling Yourself. You can market your services, but people will be hiring *you*. You must feel comfortable discussing your successes.

Diagnosing Client Needs. In some cases you will meet with your clients and they will tell you exactly what they want you to do. Sometimes they will ask you what needs to be done. And sometimes what they say they want is not what they need! Your diagnostic skills will tell you what to do in all cases.

🖫 Exhibit 2.1. Consultant Skills and Characteristics.

Rate your strengths

Skills	Strength	Needs Improvement
Prospecting and marketing		
Promoting and selling myself		
Diagnosing client needs		
Identifying mutual expectations		
Pricing projects		
Dealing with paperwork		
Understanding business data		
Designing materials		
Conducting training		
Facilitating meetings		
Depth of experience		
Breadth of experience		

Characteristics	Natural	Needs Attention
Leader		
Decision maker		
People turn to me for decisions		
Enjoy competition		
Self-confident		
Enjoy working long, hard hours		
Always plan ahead		
Self-disciplined		
Sell myself with confidence		
Financial acumen		
Reasonable risk taking		
Family support		

Which skills and characteristics need the most improvement and attention?

How will you gain necessary skills or experience?

How will you adapt to necessary characteristics that are not naturally "you"?

Identifying Mutual Expectations. The ability to lead a candid discussion with your client to reach agreement on what each of you needs, wants, and expects as a result of working together will ensure that your projects start on the right foot.

Pricing Projects. How long a project will take, how many on-site days are needed, how long it will take to design and develop the materials, and how many trips you will make to the client's location will all affect the price tag you place on a project.

Dealing with Paperwork. Organizing your office so that you will be able to locate everything that you file and developing processes to track clients, money, and work will be critical to your success.

Understanding Business Data. This book offers numerous methods for tracking your data, such as expense records, profit-and-loss statements, and revenue-projection forms. Your ability to read them, analyze them, and know what they are telling you is important for your financial health.

Designing Materials. Even if you don't design your own material, you must be able to spot quality in materials for purchase and compare the pros and cons of different models. You must be able to look at an activity and tell how much time it might take or whether it is appropriate for your client.

Conducting Training. You may not bill yourself as a trainer, but you will train in many ways. You may coach a CEO, mentor a manager, or do some one-on-one training with superintendents on the floor. Internalizing adult learning theory will ensure that you are always ready for those teaching moments.

Facilitating Meetings. You very likely will be called on to facilitate meetings for your client. Brush up on meeting-management skills as well as facilitation skills. You will be seen as a model in many situations. These skills will help you hold your own.

Depth of Experience. How deep is your experience? If you are specializing in an area, you should know all you can about it. Read your professional journals and keep up with the latest books in your area. As a specialist, you have expertise in a particular field, industry, or focus area.

Breadth of Experience. How wide is your experience? You must be enough of a generalist to know what else applies in the situation you are dealing with. You should know where you can go for help when you need it. As a generalist you will be expected to have a heavy dose of common sense to provide an outside perspective and to cut through internal politics. You will have a wide range of experience.

A balance of breadth and depth is a critical advantage your client will look for. It is also important to decide whether to present yourself as a specialist or a generalist. The more specialized you are, the more difficult it will be to obtain a wide variety of business; the more generalized you are, the less credible you may be in a potential client's eyes.

The more specialized you are, the more difficult it will be to obtain a wide variety of business; the more generalized you are, the less credible you may be in a potential client's eyes.

PERSONAL CHARACTERISTICS OF SUCCESSFUL CONSULTANTS

Consulting is a profession of contrasts and high expectations. Not only will you need to be multi-skilled, sensibly focused, knowledgeable, and widely experienced, but you will walk a fine line among personal characteristics. Your clients expect you to be confident, but not arrogant; assertive, but not pushy; intelligent, but not a nerd; personable, but not overly friendly; candid, but not critical; understanding, but not too sensitive. In addition they will want you to be creative and visionary, but at the same time logical and practical. You will need to see the big picture, but also watch out for the details that might trip you up.

This affords you quite a challenge! A client will be just as interested in your personal characteristics as in your skills. Although clients will ask you to discuss your skills, they will evaluate your characteristics.

Although clients will ask you to discuss your skills,
they will evaluate your characteristics.

ROLES YOU MAY PLAY

Although there are hundreds of roles you may play as a consultant, the following examples will give you an idea of what a client may expect of you. As a consultant you may come in at any point in a situation facing a client. Although the examples are somewhat oversimplified, they may help you decide the role that you can fill the best.

Identify the Problem. You may enter when a client knows something is wrong in general, but just cannot identify what: Morale is down, communication is poor, turnover is high, and profits are questionable. In this case, you may be asked to identify the problem. You will probably be required to gather data, interview people, study the bigger picture, recognize interfaces, and benchmark other organizations. The roles you will play include interviewer, analyzer, synthesizer, categorizer, and researcher.

Identify the Cause. You may enter when a client knows there is a problem: Sales are down; time from concept to market is too long; or defects are high. The client knows there is a problem, but does not know what the cause is. You may be asked to identify the root cause of the problem. You will need to understand the basics of problem solving, how to uncover the root cause, how to communicate with process owners, and how to challenge the status quo. You may need to have a heavy dose of expertise in the area. The roles you will play include expert resource, auditor, devil's advocate, mediator, and problem solver.

Identify the Solution. You may enter when a client knows there is a problem and has identified the cause: Sales are down because the competition has introduced a new product; time from concept to market is too long because the staff doesn't work well together; or defects are high because the supplier is unreliable. In this case you may be asked to identify a solution or solutions. You will probably need to research outside initiatives in the same or other industries. You may need to locate other resources or to coordinate and facilitate open discussion. You will need to help others identify potential ideas. The roles you will play include processor, idea generator, facilitator, and adaptor.

Implement the Solution. You may enter when a client knows there is a problem, has identified the root cause, and has determined the solution: Need to attract a new customer base; need to work better as a team; or need to improve supplier communication. In this case you may be asked to implement the solution or change. You will be expected to make things happen. If you must install the new, you may also be required to get rid of the old. You will need to deliver information and assist others to communicate effectively. You may need to supervise installations and reconfigure the work force. The roles you will play include catalyst, implementer, change agent, mentor, communicator, and coordinator.

Each of the examples given requires you to play different roles. Obviously, there is a lot of crossover, but think about your talents and which roles you could fill best. What are your strengths? What do you most enjoy doing?

Now that we've examined the skills and roles that may be required, let's look for signs that you may not be cut out to be a consultant.

SIGNS OF A MEDIOCRE CONSULTANT

In twenty years of consulting, I've observed hundreds of consultants. Many were very good and some were mediocre. You aren't starting your business to be mediocre, so here are some of the practices and characteristics that lead to mediocrity.

- A belief that being a consultant means that you can be just who you are without concern for what your clients expect and refusing to be flexible to fit their environment when necessary.
- An inability to identify practical marketing tactics or finding excuses to avoid implementing them.
- An inability to recognize an opportunity when it is slapping you in the face, for example, clients or potential clients saying, "Do you know anything about. . . ." or "Something that is really bugging me is. . . ." or "I'd like some help with. . . ." These are all cries for help. Listen! Listen! Listen! Your next project may be speaking to you!

- An insistence on using a model or solution that you are familiar with rather than creating or finding a new one that would be more appropriate.
- An insistence on doing the same things over and over, not creating new materials or trying new options.
- No desire to continue to grow and learn.
- No recognition that your consulting practice is a business.

Average is just average. Is that what you want to be?

YOUR PERSONAL SITUATION

Before you quit your job and buy your business license, take time to identify any personal situations that may make the profession difficult for you. I've listed five that are frequently identified. You may have others. The best way to discover these may be to discuss your own situation with a friend, your spouse, or a significant other.

Financing the Business

Even if you leave your present job with the promise of six months of work, there is no guarantee that you will have your next projects lined up when that income stream ends.

You may become so tied up in the project that you don't take the time to prospect for new projects. Or you may decide that you deserve some time off before you plunge into your business. In either case, you may not have a steady income following your initial project.

What can you do? Do you have savings or other cash that you can draw from during your initial start-up or later if you have no income? Can you cut back on personal or business spending? Can you obtain a line of credit from your bank? Consulting has its ups and downs. Be sure to set some money aside in a liquid investment for times when things are not going as well as you would like. It may be difficult to adjust to the fact that consulting does not produce a regular paycheck.

Consulting does not produce
a regular paycheck.

Working Alone

Leaving the hustle and bustle of an office sounds great initially, but once you spend several days in the same room without seeing anyone except the mail carrier, you may begin to go stir crazy. You may miss the opportunity to work as a team. You may miss the synergy that groups can create, and you may miss the social interactions.

What can you do? You can at least arrange to have lunch with someone once each week. You can plan to meet other consultants regularly. Even though discussion is likely to turn to work, you will still appreciate the camaraderie.

Working from Your Home

At first working from your home sounds like an ideal situation. Get up when you want to. No traffic to face. No time clock to punch. Work in your shorts and T-shirt. Listen to your favorite radio station. Brew fresh gourmet coffee in the morning. Eat a bagel while you're proofing a proposal. Walk outdoors at any time during the day. Flick the television on to hear the latest news. Pick up the kids from school. Read at your desk after everyone has gone to bed. Perfect day—right?

How about the day things don't go as well? The dog barks just as you are about to close an important sale. Your daughter spills milk on the proposal that's on its way to the post office. Your home-based office has spread to the living room. You need to leave for an important meeting and your son hasn't returned with the car. Your spouse is upset because you spend every waking hour in your office.

Both kinds of day are equally possible. You will need to face the reality of both. Think about how you can balance working at home and living at home.

Being a One-Person Company

Think about how you will feel when a client asks you how many people are in your company. Will you feel proud of being on your own or will you feel somehow inferior? How will you feel about doing your own typing, copying, errands, dusting, vacuuming?

An important factor to consider is backup support. What will you do when one of your clients is counting on you to facilitate a critical meeting and you are at home ill? Identify someone who could fill in for you. You could make a reciprocal agreement with several other consultants in your area.

Needing Family Support

Family support is critical. Starting your business will be difficult enough. You don't need your family saying, "We told you so!" when something goes wrong. Obtain 100 percent support from all immediate family members before you hang out your shingle.

The five personal situations described above are mentioned most frequently as interfering with consultants' ability to function. Each has its own solution. You must recognize the possibility of any of these problems coming up and plan your own solutions.

THE TRANSITION INTO CONSULTING

You've examined your skills, looked at your characteristics, explored the roles you may play, faced your personal situations, evaluated your talents, and have determined that you are a match for the profession. What's next?

Now decide how you will enter the profession. Will you join a large national consulting firm, join a small local firm, form a partnership, or open your own practice? Each has its advantages.

Large Firm. As a consultant for a large national firm you would be able to focus solely on consulting and generating business. Someone else would complete tax forms, hire secretarial support, and pay the rent. You would have instant name recognition and a clear career path. Although this may sound advantageous at first blush, the greatest drawback is that you might become so comfortable with your job that you would never experience the world of the independent consultant. In addition, these jobs might come with a great deal of pressure.

Small Firm. As a consultant in a small, local firm, you would experience similar advantages to those of a large, national firm. One added benefit might be that you would probably experience a wider variety of tasks and be given more responsibility sooner. If you want to travel, a drawback may be that you are often limited to working with businesses in your locality.

Partnership. As a partner with one or more other consultants, you would be able to share the burden of expenses, marketing, and the work load. The biggest drawback is the potential for conflict over numerous business and personal preferences.

These conflicts can vary from an unbalanced work load to communication to decision making.

On Your Own. As an independent consultant, you would have an opportunity to make all the decisions, do what you wanted when you wanted, and receive all the recognition. The drawback, of course, is that you would assume all the risk, be responsible for all expenses, and have no one at your level readily available with whom to discuss business plans and concerns.

The focus of this book is on the independent consultant who opens his or her own business. If you have decided this is the route you will take, you can still begin slowly.

One way would be to obtain experience as an employee in one of the national or local consulting firms mentioned above or you could work part-time or take work with you when you leave your present employer. Chapter Four provides more detail about how you can do this effectively while starting your own business.

CAUTION: BUSINESS OWNER AHEAD

So far in this chapter we have focused on what it takes to be a successful consultant. You are headed for the entrepreneurial ranks. You are about to become a business owner.

Although there is no way I can prepare you psychologically for the long hours, the endless frustrations, the demands for patience and persistence, the multitude of ups and downs, and the desperate need for planning when there is no time for planning, I can provide some suggestions for success.

Estimates generally are that 80 percent of all start-up businesses fail within five years. Responsibility for success or failure rests almost entirely with the person who started the business. You certainly do not want to be among the casualty statistics over the next year or two!

ENTREPRENEURIAL CHARACTERISTICS

Although all the experts do not agree about what makes a successful start-up business owner, the following seem to be mentioned most often.

First, you have to want to do it! Let's face it. You're tired of working for someone else and the idea of doing your own thing appeals to you—really appeals to you. You have already taken the first step. You've decided that you want to start a business, and, yes, you want to ensure that it is still around five years from now. What's next?

Self-confidence is on almost all lists. Be honest with yourself. If you don't believe in you, who will? Most consultants have a good dose of self-assurance—believing that they can do whatever they set their minds to. Before starting my business, I can remember thinking, "This is such a sure bet; I can't not succeed!"

Most entrepreneurs have a sense of urgency. They have places to go, things to do, people to see, and successes to pull off. They seem to have more energy than most people and a need to do things *now*. Interestingly enough, most require fewer than the usual eight hours of sleep each night.

They have a willingness to work hard—to do what it takes to achieve success. Long hours don't scare them. They also play hard—and competitively!

Entrepreneurs have a need to control and direct. They want the responsibility and authority that comes with owning a business. They like making decisions; they do not like being told what to do.

They have the flexibility to think differently as the need arises. They can be either creative or analytical; they can be big-picture thinkers or detail-oriented.

Maintaining a positive attitude gets entrepreneurs through the ups and downs. They truly do look at problems as challenges. They are certain a solution exists and welcome the learning that accompanies identifying the problem and solving it.

They are good decision makers. They usually rate neither high nor low in risk taking, but are good at weighing the potential outcomes. They are decisive and move forward. They don't hesitate or procrastinate. They are also willing to change a course of action if the expectations for success are less than they had hoped.

Entrepreneurs are creative problem solvers. They are conceptional thinkers and see relationships that others may not. They excel at creating order out of chaos.

They may be obsessed with quality—quality of service, quality of product, quality of a project. They are naturally committed to excellence and do not need the quality gurus to inspire them!

Good health is almost imperative, given the preceding list! I believe that it has a lot to do with positive thinking and the fact that entrepreneurs just don't have time to get sick.

Do you have what it takes to be a business owner? Can you cut it as an entrepreneur? Find out with the evaluation in Exhibit 2.2.

💾 Exhibit 2.2. Entrepreneurs: Do You Have What It Takes?

Instructions: Rate yourself on the following qualities. They represent the thinking of several authors about the requirements of a successful business owner. Spend ample time pondering these questions and answer honestly. Although this survey can only give a general picture of what it takes to be a successful entrepreneur, only you can decide if the move is right for you. Rate yourself on the following scale from 1 to 4:

1 = strongly disagree	3 = agree
2 = disagree	4 = strongly agree

Circle your answer

1.	I usually try to take charge when I'm with others.	1	2	3	4
2.	I can do anything I set my mind to.	1	2	3	4
3.	I have a high tolerance level.	1	2	3	4
4.	I believe I can always influence results.	1	2	3	4
5.	I am complimented on my ability to quickly analyze complex situations.	1	2	3	4
6.	I prefer working with a difficult but highly competent person rather than a friendly, less competent one.	1	2	3	4
7.	I can fire employees who are not producing.	1	2	3	4
8.	I am willing to leave a high-paying secure job to start my own business.	1	2	3	4
9.	I push myself to complete tasks.	1	2	3	4
10.	I can work long, hard hours when necessary.	1	2	3	4
11.	I need to be the best at whatever I do.	1	2	3	4
12.	I do not become frustrated easily.	1	2	3	4
13.	I thrive on challenges.	1	2	3	4

Exhibit 2.2. Entrepreneurs: Do You Have What It Takes?, Cont'd.

14.	I become bored easily with routine tasks.	1	2	3	4
15.	I dislike being told what to do.	1	2	3	4
16.	I have a higher energy level than most people.	1	2	3	4
17.	I have held numerous leadership positions.	1	2	3	4
18.	I have the skills and enjoy accomplishing a complex task by myself.	1	2	3	4
19.	I can change my course of action if something is not working.	1	2	3	4
20.	I am seen as a creative problem solver.	1	2	3	4
21.	I can balance the big picture and details of a business at the same time.	1	2	3	4
22.	I can predict how my actions today will affect business tomorrow and in the future.	1	2	3	4

23. I need at least _____ hours of   1 = 8 hrs   2 = 7 hrs
sleep to function effectively.   3 = 6 hrs   4 = 5 or fewer hrs

24. I have at least _____ years' of   1 = 1 yr   2 = 2 yrs
experience in the business   3 = 3 yrs   4 = 4 yrs
I will start.

25. Over the past three years I   1 = 16 days   2 = 11–15 days
have missed a total of _____   3 = 6–10 days   4 = 0–5 days
days of work due to illness.

Scoring: Total the numbers you circled

90 – 100	Go for it!
82 – 89	Good chance of success
74 – 81	Pretty risky
73 and below	Better continue to collect a paycheck

This chapter focused on the required talents and characteristics of consultants. You can see the multi-talented person a client will expect. You probably have a better picture of the drawbacks now, as well as the rewards of consulting. If you are excited by the opportunity and challenged by the adventure, you are ready to begin thinking about what you need to do to start.

Dollars and Sense

"People know the price of everything and the value of nothing."

Oscar Wilde

Determining what to charge clients is usually the most difficult decision for a first-time consultant. Yet it is a decision that must be made before you can begin to solicit business. Your client will most likely want to know, "How much will this project cost?"

There are really two issues: (1) How much money you need and (2) How much a client is willing to pay you. Although they are closely related, it is important to keep them separate in your mind. If the two amounts are relatively close or if clients are willing to pay you more than you require (what an exciting problem to have!), you'll find it easy to balance your budget. On the other hand, if you suspect that you require more than clients are willing to pay for your services, you may want to reconsider opening a consulting practice.

Let's examine each of these issues: How much money do you require? and How much should you charge for your services?

HOW MUCH MONEY DO YOU REQUIRE?

Determine how much income you will require as a consultant in one of two ways. The first way is to calculate in detail your salary, taxes, benefits, and business expenses for one year. A second way, the "3× Rule" (pronounced "three times rule"), will provide a quick estimate of your requirements.

Calculation Method

Your perceived value is one way to start. What do you believe you should make in a year? Starting here makes sense because an annual salary is the way most of us think of our value. Don't forget benefits, including insurance, retirement contributions, self-employment taxes, and vacation time. You may identify each benefit individually or simply add on 25 to 33 percent as an estimate. After that, develop a budget for running your business. Exhibit 3.1 will help you remember most of your expenses. In addition to annual expenses, you will have some one-time start-up costs. Chapter Four provides more details about these. Use Exhibit 3.1 to estimate the amounts you will need to cover your salary, benefits, taxes, and business expenses. Total these to determine how much money you will require annually.

The 3x Rule

If you don't want to take time now to identify your business expenses, the 3× Rule will give you a close estimate. The 3× Rule is used by many consulting firms to determine how much to bill clients (and in some cases how much business to generate as well) in order to pay salaries to themselves, cover overhead, and contribute to profit for the company. For example, consultants with a salary of $50,000 are expected to bill at least $150,000 each year. Does this seem excessive? Do you wonder what happens to all that money? You already know that $50,000 is earmarked for your salary. The other two-thirds pays for fringe benefits such as insurance, FICA, unemployment taxes, worker's compensation, and vacation time; overhead such as marketing, advertising, electricity, professional development, telephone, supplies, clerical support, and management; and down time—those days when consultants are traveling, off for a holiday, or in training—and for development and preparation time. The additional money also covers days that cannot be billed due to an inability to match available consultants to client dates.

If you plan to work out of a home office and you do not plan to hire support staff the first year, you might be able to whittle your requirements down to a "2× Rule," but your budget will be tight and you may experience cash-flow problems. (More about cash flow in Chapter Six.) Be cautious about playing a tight numbers game.

🖫 Exhibit 3.1. Calculating What You Require.

Your Salary for One Year   _____

Your Benefits
    Health insurance   _____
    Life insurance   _____
    Disability insurance   _____
    Retirement   _____
                   Total Benefits   _____

Taxes
    Self-employment   _____
    Social Security and Medicare   _____
    State income tax   _____
    City tax   _____
    Personal property tax   _____
                   Total Taxes   _____

Business Expenses
    Accounting, banking, and legal fees   _____
    Advertising and marketing   _____
    Automobile expenses   _____
    Books and resources   _____
    Clerical support   _____
    Copying   _____
    Donations   _____
    Dues and subscriptions   _____
    Entertainment   _____
    Equipment leases   _____
    Interest and loan repayments   _____
    Liability insurance   _____
    Licenses   _____
    Lodging (non-billable)   _____
    Materials (non-billable)   _____
    Meals   _____
    Office supplies   _____
    Postage   _____
    Professional development   _____
    Rent   _____
    Repairs and maintenance   _____
    Telephone   _____
    Travel (non-billable)   _____
    Utilities   _____

                   Total Business Expenses   _____
                   Total Required   _____

Your Circumstances

As you begin to put numbers on paper, you must also consider your personal circumstances. Are you the primary breadwinner in your family? Can someone else pick up some of the slack as you are starting your business? What can you contribute from your savings as you start your own consulting practice? (*Note:* Many experienced consultants recommend that you have a six-to-twelve-month cushion.) What work can you count on immediately? How long will it take to generate additional work?

As many companies downsize, they offer employees "consulting contracts" as part of a severance package. This may be an ideal scenario for you. It usually means that you are responsible for specific projects identified by your former employer for which you receive an amount that is somewhat less than your former salary. The projects may require less than half of your time and you can use the rest to generate and conduct other business. Generally these agreements extend for less than one year and are nonrenewable. Many budding consultants find this an ideal way to start.

HOW MUCH SHOULD YOU CHARGE?

Deciding how much to charge is difficult because you naturally feel modest and do not want to charge too much, but also cannot afford to charge too little. Here is how to decide how much to charge for your services.

Determine Typical Charges

Charges are determined by many factors. The greatest determining factor is the client: the business or industry, the size and location, the demand, and the history of consultant use. The next determining factor is the consultant: The level of expertise, the amount of experience, and the person's stature. This unique supply-and-demand situation creates a wide price range. I've worked with consultants who have charged as little as $200 per day and as much as $20,000 for a one-hour speech! So what's realistic?

The June 1996 issue of *Training and Development* reports in an article titled "What Things Cost" that the daily rates for consultants range from $35 to $7,500. Fifty-five percent of respondents to the poll reported that they charged between

$500 and $1,500 per day. Another survey conducted by the OD Network in Chicago, reported in the *ODN Newsletter* in September 1994, found rates ranging from $300 to $2,100 per day. The range of rates is broad for many reasons. For example, if you live near a university, you may find professors who consult part-time. Because they already have a full-time salary, their consulting practice is seen as "extra spending money," and they may seriously underbid you. I have met professors charging as little as $150 per day in order to gain the experience or obtain data for an article they were writing.

Also check your market area for services similar to yours but priced much lower. For example, a local mental health clinic may offer a stress-management class for $6. A community college may offer a time-management course for $15. If either of these is your specialty, you may have a difficult time convincing companies to pay $800 per day—even if you do customize the materials for them.

The client determines acceptable fee ranges. Generally, for-profit companies have more in their budgets for your services than do nonprofit organizations. Usually, the larger the company, the larger the discretionary funds available. The OD Network survey mentioned earlier found that consultants working in the corporate world charge $400 to $2,100; those in government $400 to $1,300; those in nonprofit fields $0 to $1,900; and those in church-related work charge $0 to $800. Note that these figures show a wide range as well as how those ranges change by type of client.

The larger the company, the larger the discretionary funds available.

Location of either the client or the consultant will also affect the fee charged. The OD Network study was conducted for one region only. It is safe to assume that the ranges would be different in other areas. It is natural to expect that consultants in large cities such as New York, Boston, or Los Angeles will charge more than consultants in smaller towns.

Finally, the consultant determines the fee. What expertise do you have? Is it unique or commonplace? How much experience do you have? With what kind of clients? Do you work internationally? Nationally? State-wide? or Locally? How well known are you? What perceived value do you add due to stature in the business, authored books, or university affiliations? The answers to each of these will help to determine your rate.

Determine Your Fee

Although it may be interesting to know that some consultants charge more for one day than you may presently make in a month, the real question is how to determine what you should charge.

You can determine a fee in one of two ways. You can start with the requirements you compiled and plan toward that end or you can approach the problem from the standpoint of what the market will bear.

Plan with the End in Mind. To use this method, return to your calculations to obtain the amount that you need for living and business expenses for one year. Think in terms of how much billable time is actually available. There are fifty-two weeks in a year, and you will probably take off at least two of them. In addition you must account for New Year's Day, Memorial Day, July Fourth, Labor Day, Thanksgiving, Christmas, and other holidays. This leaves about forty-nine weeks or 245 days, assuming a five-day week. Generally, you will average between two and three billable days per week or a maximum of 120 days per year, for two reasons. The first is that you will need time to run your business. You will need to market, network, write proposals, travel, bill clients, and complete many other administrative details required to manage a business. In addition you will need to develop your skills, learn new techniques, and keep up with the changes in your field as well as the industries in which you work. As a consultant you must maintain your professional edge.

The second reason it is highly unlikely that you will bill more than 120 days in one year is the difficulty of matching your clients' needs with your available days. You may find that all your clients need you the same week in September. You may need to turn down some of those billable days. Then again, you may find yourself with a week or two in December with no billable days. Exhibit 3.2 will help you to determine your actual billable days.

Let's work through an example. You have determined that you require $50,000 to live for a year. You added $20,000 for taxes, $7,500 for retirement, and $6,000 for various kinds of insurance. This brings what you will bill to $83,500.

💾 Exhibit 3.2. Actual Billable Days.

Days in a Year	365
Weekend Days	− 104
	= 261
Time Off	
Vacation, personal (5–15 days per year)	− _____
Holidays (6–12 days per year)	− _____
	= _____
Marketing (1–2 days per week)	− _____
Administrative (2–4 days per month)	− _____
	= _____
Down time (15–30 percent)	− _____
Days you expect to work	☐

Let's suppose that you will begin by working out of your home and that you expect overhead to be small for your first year, about $2,100 per month or $25,200 per year. Now the total amount that you must bill is $108,700. Because this is your first year in business, you know it will take some time to build a client base. You decide to play it safe and plan on eighty days of consulting.

Next you will divide the total dollar amount, $108,700, by eighty. That gives you a daily rate of $1,358.75. Most consultants would round that figure to $1,350 for each billable day.

You should consider one last thing. A successful business makes a profit each year. Don't confuse your salary with your business profit. A profit is your reward for business ownership and the risk that it incurs. A 10 percent profit is very respectable for a first year in business, so you may want to add $10,000 for a profit margin. This increases what you will need to bill for your first year to $118,700. Using the original eighty billable days, that amounts to almost $1,500 per day.

Does $1,500 per day sound high for your first year in the field? It may be. You may need to return to your original budget. Can you cut expenses? Could you do all your own typing instead of using a temporary service? Can you decrease the amount you require to live? For example, could you not take an expensive vacation or could you use some of your savings for living expenses? Can you increase the number of billable days? Perhaps your present employer will retain you to complete existing projects or you could work weekends to add more days. Any of these will change the equation to lower your billable rate. Use Exhibit 3.3 to calculate your consulting fee.

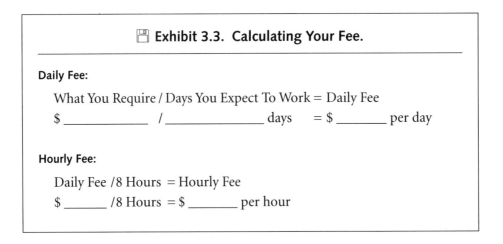

💾 Exhibit 3.3. Calculating Your Fee.

Daily Fee:

What You Require / Days You Expect To Work = Daily Fee

$ _____ / _____ days = $ _____ per day

Hourly Fee:

Daily Fee / 8 Hours = Hourly Fee

$ _____ / 8 Hours = $ _____ per hour

Although this exercise is an excellent way to determine your billable rate, you must also consider what a client will be willing to pay for your services. You certainly do not want to price yourself out of the market your first year!

Determine What the Market Will Bear. An easy way to establish your fee is to emulate your competition. Place a price on your head by determining what you believe the market will bear—that is, how much you believe your targeted clients will pay for your services. Realize that you are not charging what you are "worth" but what clients are willing to pay. In his book, *The Consultant's Calling*, Bellman (1990) says, "We are not talking about what you are worth. We are talking about what you can get for working for others. Your ultimate value is not being put on the line in this decision." This is an important distinction. Your fee does not measure your actual worth but only what clients are willing to pay for your services.

If you use this method, remember to look at your competition. As a new consultant, you may want to collect as much information as you can about what clients are paying for services and what consultants are charging for services. Don't be surprised if this information is difficult to obtain. I have found most consultants to be quite closed about what they charge. Of course you need to pay attention to the Sherman Anti-Trust Act to ensure that you will not be accused of price fixing!

If you decide to follow what the market will bear, you will want to explore some other issues to help you determine your fee. Ask yourself these questions: What's your specialty? How common is your expertise? What is unique about your experience? What industry are you targeting? What constitutes a typical consulting fee for companies in this industry? Where is your market? What is the range of fees organizations pay in this market? Who else offers similar services? What do they charge? Your answers will help you determine your rate.

Pricing Strategy

Whether you decide to plan with the end in mind, go with what the market will bear, or use a combination of the two methods, you must still select a pricing strategy. Your figures will result in a range, so you will have to determine whether to charge at the high end or the low end of the range. Experience shows that most new consultants select the lower price. They feel that if they price low they will find more contracts to "get started."

However, pricing services too low is the biggest mistake that new consultants make. Choose the high end of the range—for several reasons. First, the higher price means that you will need to accept fewer contracts. This allows you to manage your time better, giving you the flexibility to deal with all those unforeseeable things that crop up when starting a business. It also allows you to spend more time with your clients, giving them better service rather than worrying about your next contract. Charge a price that allows you to do the job with superior quality.

Charge a price that
allows you to do the job
with superior quality.

Second, your consulting rate sends a message. True or not, a higher price often is equated with higher quality. A low price may send a message that you are not worthy of important projects. A low bid may help you acquire some early projects, but may also be a reason that clients are uncomfortable hiring you again—especially if the project was not large enough to develop a solid relationship. Achieving the reputation of being the cheapest consultant in town means only that you are "the cheapest consultant in town!"

Third, if you offer what clients need, they will most likely pay the price you request without questioning it. It will be much easier to start high than to increase your rates at a later time.

SELECTING A PRICING STRUCTURE

The discussion so far has focused primarily on a daily fee. There are other possible pricing structures. Often the industry you serve or the kind of consulting you do will determine the pricing structure you choose.

Daily Rate

Training, organization development, or management development consultants typically charge by the day. That day may be six to twelve hours long depending on the task at hand. If you are conducting training that begins at 8 A.M., you will probably need to arrive before 7 A.M. to set up the room—or even set it up the night before the session. The session may last until 4:30 P.M., but participants may stay around to discuss the day with you. After they leave, you may still want to organize the room and your materials for the next day, study your notes, or examine work that was generated by the participants during the day. It may be 6 P.M. before you leave for the day. An eleven-hour day may be the norm, and you do not charge overtime for the additional hours.

Billing by the day may make you seize as many days of work as possible—even when they don't fit into your schedule well. When a day has passed without a billable client, you have lost that income potential forever. Billing by the day limits your earning power to the number of days in a year. This puts strong emphasis on days worked as opposed to results achieved. Remember that a billable day is a billable day; once it's gone, it is lost forever.

A billable day is a billable day;
once it's gone, it is lost forever.

Hourly Rate

Consulting fees charged by the hour are standard in some industries, such as computer programming and engineering. In this case, you will provide a range of hours (minimum and maximum) you expect the job to require. Travel time is not generally billed in any of the other methods of charging; it is in the hourly rate structure.

Both a daily rate and an hourly rate require the client to assume the risk for the total cost of the project. Thus, they are more typically used for training or tasks that have clearly defined time parameters and outcomes.

Fixed-Price Projects

Establishing a firm price for a complete project is how I prefer to bill. Specific results are identified for the completion of a project. Although some consultants resist this method of pricing, due to the risk involved if the price is too low, my experience shows that this is the trend. Tom Peters says, "It's a project-based world. If you're not spending at least 70 percent of your time on projects, you're living in the past" (Peters, 1997).

You may have to bid on a fixed-price basis if you work for government agencies. Responding to a Request for Proposal (RFP) from any organization may also require you to determine a fixed price for an entire project. An RFP is often used when several consultants are competing for a job.

I prefer this pricing structure for several reasons. First and most important, the client's employees can call at any time for assistance and, unlike my attorney, I won't start the timer. Second, the method is performance and results oriented. We are paid for what we accomplish. Third, this method is the best match for a custom design. Fourth, this method is better for larger contracts. Several large contracts are easier to manage than dozens of little ones.

How can you determine a price? First, estimate how much time you expect the project to require. If this is your first time with this method, you may still want to use a daily rate to find a ballpark price. With this method, you assume the risk of the total cost of the project. Ethically, you cannot charge more than the original quoted price—even if you lose money. We have lost money on a couple of projects due to poor estimating. In these situations, we have always continued to provide the highest quality work and have not disclosed our predicament to the client. This would be unprofessional. It certainly taught us good estimating skills quickly! In his book, *Million Dollar Consulting*, Alan Weiss (1992) advocates this approach and states, "If you want to make a million dollars or more in this profession, charging by time units isn't the route to get there."

Per Person

Charging by the number of participants who attend a session is another way to look at pricing. It is typically used by trainers offering public seminars. Government agencies may want you to use this type of fee structure because it more closely matches their budgeting structure. If you do choose this method, consider an up-front agreement that you will be paid for a minimum number of participants. In other words, if you require payment for a minimum of eighteen and only sixteen people attend, you will still be paid for eighteen.

Retainers

Retainers were very popular in the 1960s and 1970s, but less so today. A retainer establishes a set fee that the consultant receives on a regular basis, generally monthly. A retainer typically covers a span of twelve months. The client is assured that the consultant is available on an as-needed basis. The client and consultant determine an approximate amount of time that will be required monthly. The advantage to the consultant is a regular income; the drawback is that the consultant must plan around the needs of the client.

Conditional Fee

Some organizations pay a fixed price to a consultant on the completion of a clearly defined task. This method may be used by search firms in executive recruiting, where the conditional fee is paid only after the recruiting consultant provides the organization with four qualified candidates for a specific position.

Percentage Fee

Percentage fees are used when the financial outcome of the project is easily and clearly measurable. The consultant agrees to a percentage of the financial success of the project. This method works well for sales or marketing consultants. The client and the consultant agree that a percentage of the financial gain or savings will be paid to the consultant. A consultant can do very well with this arrangement, and the client is assured that the consultant will focus on the bottom line. A drawback to the consultant is that the results may not be measurable until some time after the project has been completed.

No matter which pricing structure you choose, you still must determine how much you require as well as how much you believe the market will bear.

OTHER PRICING DECISIONS

Many other decisions must be made around pricing. You must be clear about what you think about the following before you can discuss costs with a client.

Definition of a Day

If you have decided to charge by the day, you must determine what constitutes a day. If you attend meetings at your client's business from 10 A.M. until 3 P.M., is that one day? If you work on a project in your office from 7 A.M. until 7 P.M., is that one day? Do you count hours? Do you count calendar days? How will you define one day? Although we typically charge by the project, when we use daily rates we charge for one calendar day no matter how many hours beyond eight we work. No matter how you determine the length of a day, be sure to decide prior to working with clients.

Half-Day Events

What if a client needs you on-site for four hours and you are basing your charges on full-day rates? Should you charge half your regular rate? We recommend that you charge more than half. Why? First, you will spend the same amount of time going to and from the site. Second, you will probably spend the same amount of time in preparation. And, third, this billable day is spent! You have little chance of using the rest of the day in billable work. So, what can you do? You may wish to bill for something more than half a day's rate, but less than a full-day rate. Or you may wish to do as I do, which is to charge a full-day rate, even for a half-day event.

Different Tasks

Will you charge the same for facilitating a meeting as you will for presenting a keynote address at dinner? Being consistent in charging does not mean that you have only one fee. It does mean that you will charge all clients the same for the same work under the same conditions. Identify all of the tasks you might contract for in your consulting role and determine how and what you will charge for each.

Proposals or Sales Meetings

We do not charge for writing proposals. We see it as a cost of doing business. If we initiate a sales call we do not charge for the time or expenses. Nor do we charge if the client requests a visit and it is local (within a two-hour drive). However, if the client initiates a sales call that will require an overnight stay or air fare, we do request payment of out-of-pocket expenses. To open this discussion in a professional manner, I usually say, "Would you like us to make travel arrangements and bill you at cost? Or would you like to make the travel arrangements and let me know what they are?"

Pro Bono

Work that you complete for free is good for your business, good for the community, and good for your soul. I set aside at least fifteen days each year to do pro bono work for professional organizations such as ASTD, volunteer groups such as the American Red Cross, or schools or government agencies that cannot afford to pay. In these cases I do not charge a reduced fee. I tell them that I have only two fees: my client fee and free. The more you give, the more you get. Try it.

OTHER CHARGES

Besides your billing rate, you will incur extra charges that will be reimbursed by the client.

Travel Expenses

Travel, lodging, and meals are generally an additional charge to the client. Bill the client for the same amount you paid. It may be a common practice in other professions to tack on a "handling fee" for expenses, but it is not accepted in consulting. You will be expected to provide receipts for your expenses. If you work for government agencies, you will hear the term "per diem," which refers to a preestablished daily rate that has been determined for the city in which you are working. This fee, allowed by the Joint Travel Regulations, is expected to cover your lodging, meals, tips, and sometimes local travel. If you are traveling on a per diem basis, find out what it is prior to making your travel arrangements so that you can stay within the maximum amount allowed.

Materials

There are three possible ways to handle charges for materials that will be used during the consulting project: (1) materials can be included in your daily fee; (2) materials can be an additional charge to the client and can appear as an additional line item on the invoice; or (3) materials can be provided or produced by the client. When a contract includes many repeat sessions, you may help clients to save money by providing them with masters for the materials and allowing them to make their own copies. This saves you time and eliminates your need to transport materials for each session.

Overhead

Most consultants' fees include the cost of overhead. However, some larger firms itemize the charges for typing, data entry, editing, data analysis, and other off-site activities. Some firms also track and charge for telephone calls and other correspondence. Although it is unlikely that a start-up consultant will do that, you should be aware of this practice. If you ever find yourself competing on a daily or hourly rate basis with one of the large consulting firms, and you wonder how they can charge less than you, dig deeper. You will find that the firm's total sum will most likely be greater than yours due to all the additional charges.

Travel Time

Will you charge for travel time? A very small portion of consultants itemize travel time as billable to the client at a reduced rate. Most simply consider it a cost of doing business.

FEE INCREASES

If you believe setting your initial fees is difficult, wait until you are faced with increasing your fees. You will have many questions on your mind: "Will they pay more?" "Will I lose some of my clients?" "How do I tell them?"

I remember sitting next to the Elizabeth River with a friend trying to decide whether I should increase my fees from $750 to $800 or $900. In the end my friend convinced me to go for it!

Although I've never experienced a negative reaction to fee increases, I know that some consultants have. An increase in your fees may result in a loss of clients. However, if you give your clients enough time to adjust their budgets and you're not increasing your rate by some astronomical figure, your clients will most likely understand. A six-month notice is generally considered fair, ethical, and appropriate. We tell our clients about an increase verbally, then follow up with a written note. In addition, we include a reminder with the first invoice at the new rate. This is one time that you cannot over-communicate.

How do you know that it's time to increase your fees? You'll know when you are so busy you don't have time to increase your fees! It's a simple matter of supply and demand—or so I once thought. At one point in my career I had about twice the work I could handle, so I increased my fees. In fact, I doubled them, thinking that my projects would be cut in half and that I would break even financially with less work. That didn't happen. Instead, when I raised my fees it created a perception that I was more valuable! Raising my fees actually *increased* business.

Sometimes when you increase your rates, your proposals are bumped into a new category, requiring approval by a higher level of management. This is good because higher levels in any organization generally have larger budgets and more discretionary funds. A difference of $13,000 one way or another is not as critical to a vice president as it is to a line manager. Lesson learned? Don't underestimate yourself. If you add value, the work will be there.

If you add value,
the work will be there.

ETHICS OF PRICING

Although Chapter Nine is dedicated to the ethics of consulting, three issues about pricing ethics deserve to be mentioned here.

Determine a Consistent Pricing Structure

The highest compliment that I can receive from a client is to hear that we are ethical. The fastest way to undermine that trust is inconsistent pricing for different clients. To ensure that this does not happen, identify a clear and consistent pricing structure for all of your clients. Charging one client $900 for one day of training and another on the other side of town $1,100 for the same type of training will cause problems. Clients get together at their industry professional meetings and share what they are doing. You do not want them to discover a difference in your pricing.

Some situations do exist in which you might not charge the same for all clients or for all work, but be certain that these occasions are clearly spelled out in your pricing strategy. Be certain that you adhere to your own strategy. Two situations in which you might charge different prices follow:

1. *The work is different.* You might use a different pricing strategy for different kinds of work—one price for work done on-site and another for work done at your office. You might have a consulting fee and a training fee and perhaps a design fee that is less than either of them. You may charge a different fee for speaking engagements than for training. And, of course, if you are subcontracting with other consultants you will always charge less, as they have the burden of risk and acquired the contract with their marketing investment.

2. *The organization is nonprofit.* You may also choose to give a discount to nonprofit organizations, associations, government agencies, church or school groups, or even your favorite charity. But always identify a measurable reduction and be consistent. Why would you give one nonprofit group a 10 percent discount and another 50 percent? You may have a good reason, but being clear about your pricing strategy will help you to maintain an ethical image. Remember that your discount strategy is something that you have determined ahead of time. It is not something you negotiate with a client.

Save Bargains for Department Stores

Although we all love a sale, consulting is not a post-seasonal business. It is unethical for you to lower your rates simply because clients do not have the amount you first quoted in their budgets. How could this happen? You determine that your rates for the project will be $5,500. The client responds that there is only $4,500 in the budget for the project. It is very tempting (especially if you don't have any work lined up for the next few weeks) to say, "Okay, I'll do it for $4,500." This is one of the ways that consultants gain a bad reputation. If you can do it for $4,500, why did you ask for $5,500? Does that mean that you had $1,000 worth of fat in the proposal? It will make a client question your ethics and the ethics of all consultants.

The only way that you can lower the price of an original quote is to eliminate some of the services, so there is a true trade-off for the services you offer. For example, you might say, "We could do it at the lower price if you copy the training materials there, compile the evaluations yourself, and provide all the equipment." Or you might eliminate a more valuable service, saying, "We could do it at the lower price, but it would mean that I would not spend a day at your company interviewing people in order to customize the participant materials." When I take this approach, two things usually happen. First, I feel good about myself when I do not succumb to the monetary temptation. Second, the client usually does not want to give up the service and most often says that the money will be found someplace.

If neither of these types of suggestions work, be prepared to walk away from the project. I have walked on at least a dozen occasions. Every time the client called back to say he or she could "scrape up the money" somehow. I'd like to believe that something greater occurred. I believe that I was educating the client about appropriate consulting ethics.

Don't sell yourself short. If you find that new clients often ask you to reduce your rates, you may want to research the marketplace in which you are working. Have you priced yourself above what the market will bear? If yes, you have at least two choices. First, you may want to lower your prices. To do this you may need to decrease the services you presently provide to clients or decrease your cost of doing business. Second, you may want to locate another market in which your fees are more competitive.

Charge Higher Rates for a Specific Project

The ethics of increasing your rates are even fuzzier than those for reducing your rates. If you are up-front and candid with your client it's probably okay. Why would you raise your rates? I can think of at least two reasons: The client wants the task completed in a ridiculously short amount of time or the client insists on using you for a project that you dislike.

In either case, you are most likely justified in quoting an increased fee—especially if you are candid in your explanation to your client.

MONEY DISCUSSIONS

During discussions with your clients, you may want to take the responsibility for bringing up the topic of cost. Talking about money is difficult for some people.

Take the lead by saying, "You probably want to know how much this will cost." When I open the discussion, I often see relief on the client's face—grateful that I brought up the subject.

Sometimes during that first discussion, you may see potential complications with the project, an unusual timeline or something unique that you haven't done before. This may make it difficult to price the project on the spot. In this case, you can say, "I'm not sure of the price at this time. Let me go back to my office and put a proposal together that will outline a work plan and the cost. I will have the proposal on your desk tomorrow." This buys you time to plan the project and to price it appropriately. Don't allow yourself to be forced into providing a "rough estimate." An exact figure the next day is better for both you and the client. Naturally, you must live up to your promise to deliver the proposal and price quote when you say you will.

VALUE OF A GUARANTEE

If you are just starting your consulting practice, you might consider offering a 100 percent satisfaction guarantee. If the client is not satisfied with your work, you will return the full amount. Sound risky? It shouldn't. If you don't believe in yourself, who will? If you don't believe in your ability to meet and exceed clients' needs, perhaps you are considering the wrong profession. You should not be practicing on clients. You should know your abilities and be able to guarantee the job.

---

*If you don't
believe in yourself,
who will?*

I've offered a 100 percent money-back guarantee from my first day in the profession. Many of my first clients gave me a chance because the guarantee provided reassurance that I was confident in my ability to complete the project successfully. If I wasn't successful, they wouldn't have to pay. Since that time many have said the guarantee made the choice easy. As one of my clients from NASA said, "It was a win no matter how we looked at it!"

A guarantee does two things for you and your business. First, it makes it easier for the clients to say "yes" to you. They have nothing to lose. Either you accomplish the task that needs to be done or it doesn't cost them a thing. Second, it tells the client that you are confident and competent at what you do. What better way to begin a consulting relationship?

Establishing your fee and pricing structure may be the most difficult decisions you must make in "the business of consulting," but it's not impossible. Don't let it prevent you from moving forward.

A guarantee tells the client
that you are confident and competent
at what you do.

Starting . . .

"If you put everything off till you're sure of it, you'll get nothing done."

Norman Vincent Peale

Are you chomping at the bit to get started? That's a good sign. You are excited about tackling all the things necessary to begin your business. One of your biggest questions will be, "How much will it cost to start my consulting business?" The answer is that it will be surprisingly less than you imagine.

But there is much more to consider than start-up costs when you begin a business. You must select an accountant, determine a business structure, develop your business plan, and define your niche in the field.

Image plays a key part in how successful you will be right away. This chapter provides tips on how you can look like a million from day one—on a shoe-string budget!

This chapter also explores the age-old question, "I need project experience to be hired; how do I find a project to get that experience?" Numerous ideas are provided about how to land that first client.

SELECTING AN ACCOUNTANT

Your first task is to select an accountant. You're thinking, "Hey! Why do I need an accountant? I haven't made any money yet!" That may be true, but you have many decisions to make that will be dependent on good advice.

How do you find a good accountant? I do not recommend that you use your second cousin Joey. You are making life-changing decisions and need someone who is knowledgeable (Joey probably is), experienced (Joey may be), impartial (Joey will have difficulty), and not personally involved with you (not Joey!).

You will find a good accountant the same way you have probably found the best employees, restaurants, and barbers—by networking and asking others. Start by asking successful people, preferably other consultants, who they use for accounting. Try to identify the qualities you are looking for so that you can describe your "ideal" accountant. First, you want someone who understands what you want—even if *you're* not sure yet. Ideally you will find someone who has experience with small consulting start-ups. Interview a few accountants before you select one with whom you will work. This relationship is one of the most important to your business. It is worth the time to look for someone with whom you can partner on your most intimate business matters—money.

It is worth the time to look for someone with whom you can partner on your most intimate business matters—money.

I tried several accountants before I found one who met my needs. I wanted someone who would challenge me, keep me abreast of new tax and investment laws, and would take risks with me. I finally found the right person because I was able to describe what I was looking for in one phrase. I wanted a "creative accountant." That may seem like an oxymoron, but when I used this phrase while interviewing accountants, I could tell by their immediate response whether they understood what I was looking for. Stephanie did. She keeps me informed, suggests options, challenges my reasoning, looks for creative alternatives, and allows me to take risks within legal boundaries. Although Stephanie practices in Virginia Beach and I live in Wisconsin, the relationship works. It is a successful partnership.

The first decision your accountant can help you with is to determine the business structure that will be best for you. Many of your other decisions will be based on your business structure.

BUSINESS STRUCTURE

Selecting a business structure is one of the first and most fundamental decisions you must make. This is more critical than you might initially think, as it influences nearly every aspect of operations, such as how much you pay in taxes, the extent of your personal liability if anything goes wrong, and your ability to raise money for business expansion. There are four basic types of business structures: sole proprietorships, partnerships, corporations, and limited liability companies.

Note that some of the following information may only be valid in the United States. Check into your country's business structures and tax laws.

Sole Proprietorships

A sole proprietorship is the simplest form and creates no separate legal entity. Usually your Social Security number will serve as your company's federal taxpayer-identification number. Federal tax reporting for sole proprietorships is the easiest of the four structures, just requiring the addition of a Schedule C on which you list business income and take deductions for expenses. The structure incurs no additional tax liabilities beyond yours. Although the fact that no separate legal entity is created is usually considered an advantage, it also poses a concern. It means that any legal or tax liabilities that transpire become your personal liabilities. For example, if a client sues you for business reasons, you are personally liable and your personal assets are at risk.

Partnerships

Like sole proprietorships, a partnership is not a separate legal entity. The difference is that you will need to obtain a separate federal employer-identification number, known as your FEIN. Your partnership will file a partnership return, even though it pays no separate federal tax. The business losses and income are reported on the partners' personal tax returns. The division of profits will be governed by a partnership agreement. The decision to share equally or on a percentage basis is usually dependent on contributions of cash, experience, property, labor, and perhaps even reputation or earning power of each partner. Legally you and your partners are all personally responsible for liabilities incurred by any of the other partners or the partnership as a whole. Because so many terms must be spelled out in the partnership agreement, for example, the rights and obligations of each partner or what happens if one partner dies, a partnership can be more complicated than it may initially appear.

Corporations

Corporations differ from the first two structures in that they are separate legal and tax entities. Your personal liability is limited if the corporation is sued. Corporations are formed when individuals invest assets to create equity. To incorporate you must file articles of incorporation, create corporate bylaws, and fulfill other state requirements. Stock must be issued, even if you are the sole shareholder. The corporate structure that you are most familiar with is the "C" corporation, which is required to pay income taxes separate from you and the other shareholders.

A subchapter-S corporation (commonly called an "S corp") is an option for smaller groups. This special structure is available to U.S. organizations of thirty-five or fewer shareholders. There are other guidelines, which your accountant will share with you. One of the advantages of the S corp is that you will avoid double taxation on income to the corporation and dividends to you. The income is passed through to the shareholder (you), which you report on your personal return. By the way, both corporate structures require you to submit annual paperwork.

I usually recommend the S corp for a start-up consulting business. It has all the legal protection without much added expense. If you later decide to bring others into your business, the documentation is in place.

Limited Liability Companies

This relatively new business structure is currently permitted in forty-seven states. A limited liability company (LLC) has the limited liability of a corporation, but the flexibility and tax status of a partnership. An LLC must file articles of organization and an operating agreement with state authorities. Tax reporting is similar to a partnership, but liability is limited to the assets of the LLC. Within a year or two, if not by the publishing date of this book, all states will permit LLCs.

Because choosing the right business structure is essential for maximizing your success, it is a choice you will want to make with expert advice. Call your accountant.

BUSINESS PLANS

You will need to prepare a business plan. Unless you will try to woo investors, it can be quite simple. Your business plan allows you to put everything that is in your head on paper in an organized way. This will help you stay focused on what is important to you. View your business plan as a working document that you refer to regularly. Make it work for you. Later, as you make new business decisions, you can return to your plan to identify what you might change, how to go about changing, and how it might affect the rest of your business.

View your business plan as a working document that you refer to regularly.

What should you include in your business plan? At a minimum you will want to include a business description, marketing plan, management plan, and financial plan. The following questions will lead you through as you develop a business plan.

Business Description

Begin by describing the business, answering the following questions:

- What's the name of the business? The address? Telephone and fax numbers?
- Who is the owner(s)?
- What's the business structure and, if incorporated, where?
- What information is important about the start of this business, for example, is it a new business or an expansion of an existing business? What was the start-up date?
- What specific activities does the business do to raise revenue?
- What services or products will it provide? What is the mission of your business?
- Why do you believe your business will succeed?
- What relevant experience do you bring to the business?

Marketing Plan

You can use the following questions to develop a simple marketing plan:

- What are the demographics of your expected client base?
- What is the size of your potential market? What percent do you expect to penetrate?
- Who is your competition? How does your product or service differ from theirs? What experience do they have?
- What is your pricing strategy and structure? How does your pricing strategy and structure differ from your competitors'?
- How will you market yourself?

If you want something more detailed, use the format in Chapter Five.

Management Plan

Answer these questions about how you plan to manage your business:

- Who are the key players in the business? What are their duties, compensation, and benefits?
- What professional support will you use, such as attorney, accountant, or banker?
- What banking services will you use and where? What process will you use to establish credit?

Financial Plan

Answer the following questions, capturing the answers on Exhibits 4.1 through 4.5:

- What assumptions are you making as a basis of the plan, such as market health, start-up date, gross profit margin, required overhead, payroll, and other expenses?
- What expenditures will you require for start-up?
- What are your cash-flow projections for each month of your first year? What are your three-year cash-flow projections?
- Where do you expect to find financing and under what terms? How will the money be used, for example, overhead, supplies, marketing?
- What is your personal net worth as displayed in a financial statement?

💾 Exhibit 4.1. Start-Up Expenses.

	Estimated Cost
Furniture	
Desk and chair	$_____
Filing cabinet	$_____
Bookcases	$_____
Table	$_____
_____	$_____
_____	$_____
Equipment	
Computer	$_____
Software: _____	
_____	
_____	$_____
Printer	$_____
Copier	$_____
Typewriter	$_____
Fax machine	$_____
Adding machine	$_____
Calculator	$_____
Telephone system	$_____
Answering machine	$_____
Postage scale	$_____
Postage meter	$_____
_____	$_____
_____	$_____
Office Supplies	
Stationery	$_____
Paper: Fax	$_____
Printer	$_____
Special	$_____
Three-hole punch	$_____
Pens, pencils	$_____
Tape, glue, other adhesives	$_____
Scissors, rulers, misc.	$_____
Seminar Supplies	
Pocket folders	$_____
Three-ring binders	$_____
_____	$_____
_____	$_____
Marketing Supplies	
Business cards	$_____
Brochures	$_____
Pocket folders	$_____
_____	$_____
_____	$_____

💾 Exhibit 4.2. Budget Format.

Net Salary for One Year _____

Benefits
    Health insurance _____
    Life insurance _____
    Disability insurance _____
    Pension plan _____
    Retirement _____
                  Total Benefits _____

Taxes
    Self-employment _____
    Social Security and Medicare _____
    State income tax _____
    City property tax _____
    Personal property tax _____
                  Total Taxes _____

Business Expenses
    Accounting, banking, legal fees _____
    Advertising and marketing _____
    Automobile expenses _____
    Books and resources _____
    Clerical support _____
    Copying and printing _____
    Donations _____
    Dues and subscriptions _____
    Entertainment _____
    Equipment leases _____
    Insurance _____
    Interest and loans _____
    Licenses _____
    Meals _____
    Office supplies _____
    Postage _____
    Professional development _____
    Professional fees _____
    Rent _____
    Repairs and maintenance _____
    Resources _____
    Salaries (employees) _____
    Seminar expenses _____
    Taxes _____
    Telephone _____
    Travel _____
    Utilities _____
                  Total Business Expenses _____
                  Total Required for One Year _____

▣ Exhibit 4.3. First-Year Cash-Flow Projection.

	Jan	Feb	March	April	May	June	July	Aug	Sept	Oct	Nov	Dec
Revenue												
Total Revenues												
Expenses												
Accounting/banking/legal												
Advertising/marketing												
Automobile												
Benefits												
Books/resources												
Clerical support												
Copying												
Donations												
Dues/subscriptions												
Entertainment												
Equipment leases												
Interest												
Insurance												
Licenses												
Lodging												
Materials												
Meals												
Office supplies												
Postage												
Professional dev.												
Rent												
Salaries												
Taxes												
Telephone												
Travel												
Utilities												
Total Expenses												
Monthly Cash Flow												
Cumulative Cash Flow												

▯ Exhibit 4.4. Three-Year Projection.			
	Year 1	Year 2	Year 3
Total Revenue	_____	_____	_____
Expenses:			
Salaries	_____	_____	_____
Benefits	_____	_____	_____
Taxes	_____	_____	_____
Marketing	_____	_____	_____
Administrative	_____	_____	_____
Total Expenses	_____	_____	_____
5 Percent Inflation	_____	_____	_____
Contribution After Inflation	_____	_____	_____

Although this may seem like a lot of work, the result will be worth it. Keep your business plan handy when making decisions. At the very least, check your business progress against your original plan quarterly. Your business plan will keep you focused.

*Your business plan
will keep you focused.*

START-UP COSTS

Now you will need to determine whether you have the money to start or to expand what you are already doing.

Start-Up May Cost Less Than You Think

Consulting start-ups usually fit into the low-cost category because starting a consulting practice can be surprisingly inexpensive. Exhibit 4.1 lists everything you need to start. As you review the list you might be thinking, "I already have a computer. I could use the fax services at the copy center down the street. It can't be that

---
🖫 Exhibit 4.5. Personal Financial Statement.

Assets
   Cash   _____
   Savings accounts   _____
   Stocks, bonds, and other securities   _____
   Accounts, notes   _____
   Life insurance (cash value)   _____
   Rebates, refunds   _____
   Autos, other vehicles   _____
   Real estate   _____
   Vested pension plan or
      retirement accounts   _____
   Other assets   _____

                       Total Assets   _____

Liabilities
   Accounts payable   _____
   Real estate loans   _____
   Other liabilities   _____

                   Total Liabilities _____

    Total Assets Less Total Liabilities = Net Worth _____

---

expensive to have stationery and business cards printed. And I could work out of my home office initially." As you total the expenses on Exhibit 4.1, you may find that you could start with as little as $3,000.

Home Offices Offer Advantages

Because few clients will visit you at your office, working out of your home is a wonderful option. Just remember that it will take discipline to stay focused on writing your marketing letters instead of watching television, to continue to pay the bills rather than visit the refrigerator. A home office offers financial advantages because you will be able to deduct a proportionate amount of your home's utility costs, taxes, or rent. Keep in mind that the IRS may require proof that your home office is used exclusively for business. Also, a home office is sometimes a red flag that alerts the IRS to an audit, with potential tax implications.

Given all the ways that you can reduce start-up expenses, the cost of starting a consulting business should not deter you. My only caution is this: Do not cut corners. Your professional image is at stake right from the start.

YOUR NICHE

The opportunities available to you as a consultant are so broad that you must narrow the choices. Narrowing your choices will help you be more efficient and will ensure that you can achieve depth in an area. Some of this will come naturally due to your skills and the experiences you have had. Other decisions may be dependent on the kind of lifestyle you have chosen, for example, whether you wish to travel.

As you narrow your choices, you will define your niche or what service you will offer and to whom. There are many ways to define your niche. Consider three things: (1) the work you will do, (2) the type of client you will serve, and (3) the location where you will work.

The Work You Will Do

You probably already know what work you will do, but be aware of other opportunities for future growth. You may define your work by the *role that you play,* for example, trainer, facilitator, coach, technical advisor, process consultant, content expert, or resource.

You may define your work by the *level of the organization* with which you will work, that is, front-line employees, first-level supervisors, managers, or executives.

You may define your work by your *topic expertise,* for example, team building, time management, leadership, computer programming, mergers, investing, or regulatory laws.

You may also define your work by the *structure of the groups* with whom you work, for example, teams, intact work groups, or individuals.

Figure out what you do that defines your niche.

The Type of Client You Will Serve

Determine the type of clients you will serve by considering the general category, the industry, special situations, and the organizational size.

Decide whether you want to work in the for-profit or nonprofit organizational category. Within the for-profit sector you can consider manufacturing, service, and so on. Within the nonprofit sector you can consider associations, educational institutions, local, state, or federal government agencies, or others in the public sector.

You can further narrow your niche by focusing on a specific industry. If you have decided to work in the for-profit service sector, you may narrow that down even more by selecting health care, hospitality, or finance. Focusing on a small number of industries can build your credibility in each.

You may choose to work with organizations that have special situations. These could include small, family-owned businesses, start-up businesses, merged organizations, or high-growth businesses.

The size of organization on which you focus provides you with credibility to other organizations of like size. You may decide to work only with Fortune 500 firms. You may decide to work only with small organizations. I consider a small organization as one with one hundred or fewer employees, a medium organization as one with one hundred to two thousand employees, and a large organization as one with over two thousand employees. You may also consider the organization's revenue. In some cases, the size measurement is industry specific. Hospitals, for example, measure their size by number of beds.

Now is the time to decide what type of client you will serve that will define your niche.

The Location Where You Will Work

Although this may be the easiest to understand, it is not always the easiest to define. It may be difficult because your industry is broad-based, such as the hospitality industry, which can be found almost everywhere. Location refers more to your preference than anything and could be defined as local, state-wide, regional, national, or international.

What location will define your niche? However you define your niche, ensure that it is broad enough to have enough clients, yet narrow enough to provide focus for you.

YOUR IMAGE

Your image is the most important marketing asset you have. In fact, as you start, your image is a critical attribute of your business as a whole. You do not have products to display; you do not have clients to brag about you; you do not have experiences to discuss. All that you have is *you* and the image you present. Therefore, it is imperative that you invest in making it all that it can be.

Here's some good news: You can look like a million on a shoe-string budget right from day one! The secret? Ensure that everything you do reeks of quality. Nothing should leave your office unless it looks impeccable, sounds professional, and feels flawless. Quality should touch all the senses.

---

*You can look like a million
on a shoe-string budget
right from day one!*

If you send a letter, it should exude quality in how it looks, sounds, and feels.

- *Looks.* It should be aligned on the paper correctly. The type should be dark black, printed with a new ribbon. The stamp and envelope label should be affixed straight.

- *Sounds.* The letter should be error-free. It should be written using correct grammar. The tone should send the message you desire. It should be written for the interest of the reader. If possible, the letter should begin with the word "you."

- *Feels.* The letter should be printed on the highest grade paper money can buy. The reader should feel the quality in the paper. If you need to save money, the pennies you will save by buying second-grade paper will not be worth the savings.

Printed materials that represent your business should also be done with quality in mind. If you own a copier, buy the best that you can afford. When you make copies, be certain that they don't pick up the dirt specks from your copier's glass. What's the secret? Clean your copier glass often with a glass cleaner. If you use the services of a local copy shop, build a relationship with the manager and employees. Let them know how important it is that your copies be clean, straight, and on high-quality paper.

What else can you do to look like a million? The following quick ideas will help. Keep your eyes open for other ideas and add them to your list.

- Use a professional to design your stationery and business cards. If you can invest in an original logo now, do so. The investment may seem high at this time, but it will pay off very quickly. Your paper products speak first for you. A professional design says, "I'm serious about my profession!"

- Design a professional-looking fax cover page. Exhibit 4.6 can be used as a model.

- Use overnight express carriers to send all proposals and important communication to clients.

- Clip documents with gold paper clips.

- If you are working from your home, be sure to have a second telephone line installed immediately. It may be cute if your three-year-old answers the phone when Aunt Sadie calls, but it's not cute if the vice president of human resources calls to ask a question about your proposal.

- Ensure that your invoices are complete, correct, and businesslike. Help your business appear bigger by using a numbering system that begins with a number that is greater than one. You could simply start with 301. Or you could present a series of numbers such as 13-076-99. The middle number is the sequential number of the invoices; the last number is the year; and the first number is just for luck!

- Use your answering machine like voice mail. First, invest in a high quality machine that is dependable, allows you to obtain messages from remote locations, and does not play a charming chime while the client awaits the tone. Change your message daily to encourage callers to leave a message. Smile when recording your message; the feeling comes through. Say something like, "Hello! You've reached the voice mail of Annie Traner. Today is Thursday, October 30, and I will be away from the office. I will check for messages today, so please leave your name and telephone number. I look forward to speaking with you and hope yours is a great day!"

Exhibit 4.6. FAX Form.

ebb associates inc
box 657
portage, wi 53901
608-742-5005
608-742-8657/FAX

ebb associates inc
box 8349
norfolk, va 23503
757-588-3939
757-588-3939/FAX

Fax To: _____

From: _____

Date: _____

Location: _____

Location: ❑ WI Office ❑ VA Office

Total Pages: _____
(Including Cover)

In addition to the above ideas, you will want to think about the image you project in general. We wanted to project a subtle professional image. We wanted to speak quietly, but professionally. To express this image, we chose to use all lowercase letters in our name. We carried out the theme further by printing gray on gray.

What image do you want to project? Many things will play a part in this: the name of your company, the graphics you choose, your title, the color and style of paper, the color of the ink, the style of brochure you distribute, the content of your marketing pieces, and the tone of your correspondence. Every interaction you have with your clients will express your image. Make sure it's the one you want.

EXPERIENCE

Remember when you were looking for your first job. It seemed that every job required experience, but how could you get experience without a job? It was a crazy circle: You needed experience to get a job, and you needed a job to get experience. Well, you may feel as if you are in that same place as you look for your first consulting project, and may be asking yourself: "I need experience to get a project, but how do I get a project to get experience?" Landing your first client can be easier than you think if you plan ahead, expand your networking, and identify creative options.

Plan Ahead

It usually takes one to six months from the day you first speak with an organization until the day you begin the project. This means that you must decide to either maintain an income while you are establishing yourself or live off money you have saved for the start-up period of your business.

Your planning should include your present employer. A common way to transfer from your present job to consulting is to have your current employer become your client. You must plan this carefully. Identify which projects you could complete, list the benefits for your employer to utilize your services, and allow enough time for your employer to accept this idea. Of course, the risk you run is that your employer may not agree with your plan. This may put you in a difficult situation until your final employment date.

Another way your present employer could assist with your transition is to allow you to work part-time while you use the rest of your time for business start-up. If your employer is gracious enough to allow this to happen, make certain that you give your part-time work your full attention. It may be very difficult to focus on the same old job when you are starting an exciting new adventure. Remember, your employer is doing you a favor; you owe the company 110 percent in return.

Expand Your Networking

Before you leap into a start-up, examine your network. Have you maintained an active network of professional contacts? If not, give yourself at least six months to build this network before starting your consulting practice.

Join professional associations and attend their meetings to identify organizations that might use your services. A word of caution, however. There is no greater turnoff to a corporate manager than to be accosted by a wanna-be consultant at a professional meeting. Do not ask for work or make appointments at the meeting. So what's the point of this suggestion?

Attend meetings with plans to meet people who may use your services. Most people are attending for business-related reasons, so it will be appropriate for you to initiate conversations about the projects in which they are involved. Find topics about which you both enjoy talking. Then the next day follow up with a note expressing a common interest, your pleasure at meeting him or her, or some other theme that was a result of your discussion. *Be sincere.* If you cannot be sincere, forget it. You will appear pushy and hungry. A test of your sincerity is whether you want to follow up, even though you sense that there is no potential project at the present time. The key phrase here is "at the present time." True networking is an investment in the future. Follow your note with a phone call to set a date for lunch or a meeting to explore opportunities or to simply learn more about the organization.

Identify other networking opportunities that can move you toward your goal, including the following:

- Make a list of everyone you know who could lead to business opportunities. Then follow up with a telephone call or a note.
- Volunteer to make presentations at local, state, and national conferences and meetings.
- Identify organizations that might use your services. Request fact-finding meetings with some of the decision makers.
- Take other consultants to lunch to gather ideas for identifying business contacts.
- Search your local newspapers for people you would like to meet.

Chapter Five covers the topic of marketing once you are in business; however, many of the ideas in the chapter can be used as you network prior to starting your business. But be sure to expand your networking list before you begin to count on a full-time salary from consulting.

Identify Creative Options

The most creative tactic I used to break into the consulting business was to work part-time for a small consulting company for three months without pay. I agreed not to contact their clients and to work as an employee under their corporate name. It was a true win-win for both of us. I was able to observe the business generation (finding clients) and billable (serving clients) processes in action and to gain experience with actual clients that I could use as references. They acquired a skilled trainer who added value to their business, worked without pay, and would not pirate their clients. Because I worked part-time, I could implement what I learned to build my own business during my off hours.

If you don't want a long-term arrangement like mine, you can provide pro bono work for community, government, or nonprofit organizations. These organizations usually have limited funds and appreciate the services that you can provide. This can be the beginning of your list of clients served.

You could also subcontract full or part-time with a large training firm that certifies trainers or you could subcontract with other consulting firms. The first could be an easy route, especially if you have been certified to conduct training programs for the organization while employed at your present company. The drawback, however, will be conducting repetitive training material. The second may provide more options in projects or actual consulting. The drawback here is that you must suppress your own ego to represent the prime firm's name. Drawbacks for both are that you will bill about one-third your typical billable rate. The advantages are that you will have an income and will be able to build your own business while working part-time in the field.

If you're looking for something more full time, you could join an existing firm to gain experience. The obvious drawback is that it continues to put off even longer the opportunity to begin your own consulting business.

Although any of these ideas can serve as quick starts to becoming a consultant, some may also slow the process of starting your own business. Only you can weigh the pros and cons of each start-up tactic. Only you can weigh the advantages of finding work versus finding the work you want. Only you can make the final decisions. Exhibit 4.7 will help you think of everything you need to make decisions for a successful start-up.

💾 Exhibit 4.7. Start-Up Checklist.

- ❑ Describe the business, its services, and its products
- ❑ Identify your market
- ❑ Analyze your competition
- ❑ Assess your skills
- ❑ Name your business
- ❑ Determine your financial requirements (budget) and your pricing structure
- ❑ Identify start-up costs
- ❑ Select an accountant
- ❑ Determine business structure
- ❑ Check on zoning laws, licenses, taxes
- ❑ Select location
- ❑ Develop a business plan that includes:
    - ❑ business description
    - ❑ marketing plan
    - ❑ management plan
    - ❑ financial plan
- ❑ Select banker, attorney, and insurance agent
- ❑ Arrange for financing (or set aside capital for a worst-case scenario)
- ❑ File legal documents to register your business

If you really want to start your own consulting firm, do it now. If you don't, a year from now you will wish you had started today.

---

*A year from now you will
wish you had started today.*

. . . And Staying in Business

"None of the secrets of success will work unless you do."

A fortune cookie

Starting your business is the first difficult step. The second is staying in business. Staying in business as a consultant means that you have a continuous flow of clients. In his book, *The Secrets of Consulting,* Gerald M. Weinberg (1985) states, "The best way to get clients is to have clients." That is a very true statement. Unfortunately, it is not of much value to you if you have just started your business!

So how do you "get" clients so that you "have" clients? Obviously, you cannot just sit back with your stack of business cards on your desk and wait for the phone to ring! You may be the best consultant in the world, produce the best materials, know the most innovative solutions, provide the best service, and be the most knowledgeable in your field. However, if no one knows about you, what are your chances of having clients? Slim to none! So you must let people know that you are available for consulting. You must market your products and services. You must promote yourself. As the fortune cookie says, you must work at it.

A successful business can be measured by an adequate supply of clients, a professional image, and an ethical reputation. Each requires your attention and energy.

All three will happen at the same time and they will all happen all of the time. Everything you do will affect your business success, as measured by your clients, your image, and your reputation.

Chapter Four addressed your image. Chapter Nine addresses building an ethical reputation. This chapter addresses how marketing will ensure that you have an adequate flow of clients to stay in business.

You must promote yourself.

Consultants must be marketing-oriented. In the beginning you may need to market yourself tirelessly, using every tactic that is at your disposal. If the term "marketing" scares you, think in terms of simply putting the word out that you are in business. You must get the word out. You *must* promote yourself.

This chapter helps you prepare a simplified marketing plan and explores marketing with little or no money. One hundred thirteen marketing tactics listed here will stimulate your creativity as you explore your own ideas to keep yourself in front of your clients. The chapter will help you plan the most efficient and effective networking activities and show you how the dreaded "cold call" can be fun when you warm it up and refocus your attitude.

This chapter gives you advice and suggestions for staying in business once you've started.

A MARKETING PLAN

More volumes must have been written about marketing your professional services than about any other topic. The topic of marketing can be pretty complicated. You may find yourself reading about marketing goals, objectives, strategies, tactics, promotions, and practices. You may read about the marketing mix. Some marketing experts discuss the "four P's" of the marketing mix: product, price, place, and promotion. Other experts discuss the "eight P's and an S": product, price, place, promotion, positioning, people, profits, politics, and service. In addition you will read about advertising, public relations, and media. Then there are discussions about personal versus impersonal promotion or direct versus indirect marketing. You can read about personal selling, client-centered marketing, leveraging your clients—well, you get the idea.

Right now you do not need a degree in marketing. You must find out how to put the word out that you have consulting services to offer. Although this may seem like an overwhelming task, and one you would rather skip, don't be tempted. Developing a marketing plan is critical if you are to stay in business.

You may say, "What? Another plan?" The answer is yes. Your marketing plan will convert your ideas and intentions into commitment and action. Your marketing plan will guide you through the year so that the important task of marketing is never pushed to the back burner.

You must put your plan in writing. A written plan puts discipline into your ideas, enables you to measure success, and provides data for future use.

We touched on a marketing plan in Chapter Four when you prepared a business plan. You have two choices: (1) If you went through that exercise and have the information, you can now use it as input to this more specific marketing plan or (2) If you did not spend time yet, you can use this process to develop a more specific marketing plan and slip it into your business plan.

Format for a Marketing Plan

A marketing plan can become quite complex. If you have never written one before, the format presented here is a simplified version. Exhibit 5.1 will take you through the eight easy steps. You will find that marketing is a combination of intuition and logic. The eight-step format will move you through the process comfortably. It will ensure that your resulting marketing plan does what it is supposed to do—put your name out there!

"Marketing is a combination of intuition and logic."

1. Analyze the Present. Because you're just starting, there is not much to analyze. However, a year from now when you make comparisons, you will want to ask these questions:

- How am I perceived in the marketplace?
- How do I compare to my competition?
- What's happening to revenue and profits?
- How satisfied are my customers?
- How do customers, colleagues, and competitors describe me, my performance, and my results?

```
┌─────────────────────────────────────────────────────────────────┐
│              🖫 Exhibit 5.1. Marketing Plan.                      │
│  ───────────────────────────────────────────────────────────     │
│                                                                   │
│   1. Analyze the present.                                         │
│                                                                   │
│                                                                   │
│   2. Clarify your strategy.                                       │
│                                                                   │
│                                                                   │
│   3. Set measurable six- to twelve-month goals.                   │
│                                                                   │
│                                                                   │
│   4. Select marketing tactics to accomplish your goals.           │
│                                                                   │
│                                                                   │
│   5. Identify resources.                                          │
│                                                                   │
│                                                                   │
│   6. Develop an annual marketing plan.                            │
│                                                                   │
│                                                                   │
│   7. Implement your plan.                                         │
│                                                                   │
│                                                                   │
│   8. Monitor your results and adjust as needed.                   │
│                                                                   │
└─────────────────────────────────────────────────────────────────┘
```

Responses to these questions will guide you as you focus on whether you project the image you desire, whether you have the competitive edge you desire, whether you are as financially successful as you desire, whether you meet your clients' expectations, and whether you have the reputation you desire.

If you have been in business for more than a year, complete this subjective analysis. If you are just starting, imagine your future. Alan Kay often says in his speeches, "The best way to predict the future is to invent it." Next year, you will have something to analyze. Today, each of your answers may still be described as your preferred future—the one you are inventing!

2. Clarify Your Strategy. Where is your business heading? You have already completed some analysis in the first chapters. Chapter Eleven will take you through a visioning exercise that may also help to clarify this question. Some questions you might ask now include:

- What size company do I want to serve?
- What geographical area will I serve?
- Will I work for government, nonprofit, or for-profit organizations?
- In what industry will I specialize?
- Will I serve groups or individuals?
- Will I serve special situations such as start-ups or mergers?
- What projects do I want to conduct?

Your answers will reflect the kind of business you wish to develop. These questions will help you generate a list of potential customers with whom you want to do business.

Your strategy might be to focus on medium to large financial institutions located along the East Coast that are facing mergers and need assistance working toward efficient, shared visions of the future.

3. Set Measurable Six- to Twelve-Month Goals. You know how important goal setting is. Be specific. Make sure you can measure yours and add time limits to them. Here are some examples:

- Generate $40,000 in repeat business from 7/1 to 1/31.
- Generate $60,000 in new business from 7/1 to 1/31.

- Acquire three new clients by 2/28.

- Acquire one new client in the banking industry by 2/28.

- Present at one new conference in the next calendar year.

4. Select Marketing Tactics to Accomplish Your Goals. Generally, advertising and direct mail do not work very well for promoting consulting, but there are hundreds of other things you can do.

This is where the fun begins. We have listed one hundred thirteen self-promotional tactics in this chapter. Use some of them or, if you prefer, use the list to spark your own tactics. Tactics are actions, including anything from cold calls to hot presentations, that put your name in front of potential clients. Examples include actions such as these:

- Make twenty-five contacts in the banking industry.

- Submit proposals to at least three new conferences.

- Offer to write another ASTD *Info-Line.*

5. Identify Resources. There is a cost to marketing. Whether you speak at conferences, write letters to the local newspaper, make calls to potential customers, purchase magazine advertising, publish a newsletter, or rent a booth at a trade show, there is a cost. You must weigh the cost and the benefits to determine if a particular marketing strategy makes sense for you.

But resources mean more than money. Resources can also mean people who can provide you with information or assistance. For example, you may have targeted a certain industry on which you would like to concentrate. You could publish an ad in one of the industry's trade journals. Or, you could go to lunch with someone you know in the industry to brainstorm ideas for approaching organizations within the industry.

6. Develop an Annual Marketing Plan. Your marketing activities will be more appealing if you break them down into small steps. For example, if you have chosen ten potential clients with whom you have a speaking relationship and you have decided you would like to focus on them in an attempt to turn them into clients within the year, part of your plan might look like this.

- Ask Wisconsin staff to help identify ten clients by July 5.
- Research the clients by July 15.
- Brainstorm potential mailing content with Edie.
- First mailing out August 5.
- Second mailing with article September 5.
- Follow-up phone call September 20.
- Autumn greetings October 8.

Exhibit 5.2 provides a layout for your marketing calendar. Notice that you can track the dates and the expected cost of each month. You can tell at a glance what you intend to do each month, where your focus is, and which months are heavy or light in activities.

7. Implement Your Plan. There is not much to say here. You've planned the work; now work the plan. Don't fall behind. Marketing results may not show up for six months. You cannot go back to fix anything that was not implemented six months ago.

8. Monitor Your Results and Adjust as Needed. Although a plan provides you with your best guess at the moment, you may need to adjust at times. For example, you may have focused your business on small companies. After you start you may find that the demand was there but the revenue was not sufficient. Perhaps you will need to refocus your client mix. You may add some medium-sized companies to boost the revenue. This will be a portion of your analysis before you develop your next marketing plan.

Ways to Develop a Marketing Plan for Free

Most business schools require their marketing majors to develop full marketing plans. Students usually write plans for the school itself or for nonprofit agencies connected to it. Most would rather write a marketing plan for a real business.

Two things will make this a successful experience for you. First, allow enough time. Writing the plan will probably be a long process occurring over a full semester. You will want to speak with the professor the semester before. Second, stay involved. Your input will be critical. You will need to provide the correct data so the plan will be based on accurate assumptions. In addition, your involvement will increase the

Exhibit 5.2. Annual Marketing Plan.

Marketing Activity for 1999	Jan	Feb	Mar	April	May	June	July	Aug	Sept	Oct	Nov	Dec
Dates												
Cost												
Total Budgeted Costs												

enthusiasm of the students and the professor. Even if the plan is less than perfect due to the students' inexperience, you may receive good advice from the professor.

SURPRISING BUT PRACTICAL THOUGHTS ON MARKETING

You may not feel comfortable about marketing, but the following thoughts will put you at ease and help you think of more ideas on your own.

Market All the Time

The drawback with a calendar of marketing activities is that it suggests that there are certain days of the month that you will be marketing and that there are certain days that you won't. The truth is that you are marketing all the time. Every experience with every client, every conversation with a colleague, every visit to a professional meeting, every comment to a friend is a marketing event. You are selling yourself. As a consultant, you represent your product or service. People around you are making decisions (subconsciously at least) about whether they can or will use your services.

*The time to market
is all the time.*

"The time to market is all the time" also means that you must religiously complete the marketing activities on your calendar. You may find yourself too busy with a current project to complete the marketing event that you had planned (for example, contacting two organizations in the next city or going to lunch with a colleague). Yes, you must complete the project, but if you tell yourself that you are too busy to complete the marketing also, you will come to the end of the busy project and not have another project to be busy on! Yes, the time to market is all the time. And the most important time to market is when you are too busy to market!

*The most important time
to market is when you are
too busy to market!*

Keep Yourself in Front of Your Clients

You can do this in three ways. First, you can physically be in their presence. When working on site, I frequently pop in on the CEO, president, HR director, or the person who hired me, even if we were not scheduled to meet. I'm sure some of you shudder at my lack of formality, but it represents who I am. I can get away with this. You may need to schedule meetings. The point is—make time for them.

Second, you can keep yourself in front of your clients with permanent, practical year-end gifts. We always look for something unique, something special. We have gained a reputation for creative gifts. For example, one year we sent miniature mugs filled with gold paper clips. They were high quality, useful, and put our logo on everyone's desk every day.

Third, you can keep yourself in front of your clients by ensuring that things periodically go across their desks, for example, articles, notes of interest, books, announcements, cards, seasonal greetings, or even cartoons! Find a reason. When someone joins our firm, we send a special announcement. For example, when Garland joined our firm, we sent a miniature chalk board and chalk with the message, "Chalk another one up for ebb associates. . . ."

Have a Strategy

Well, that certainly isn't rocket science! True! You must determine the kind of client on whom you will focus. The second step of your marketing plan is critical. Do not skip it!

You must have a strategy for several reasons. The most important is so that you know where to focus your energy. If you have decided to focus on large businesses as your niche and you continue to do work with the federal government, you may work the same number of days but may not reach the financial goals you set. You will learn from that experience.

Even with a strategy, many consultants stray from it and get their business into trouble. So it is not enough to have a strategy—you must also pay attention to it. Besides, if you do not have a strategy, how will you know when you stray from it?

Go for the Big Fish; You'll Spend the Same Time Baiting the Hook

When I started my business I decided to focus on medium- to large-size businesses. This strategy is one of the best decisions I ever made. Many new consultants focus on small businesses as their first targets, perhaps because large organizations are more intimidating. In general, small businesses have smaller training and consulting budgets. Because the decision to hire a consultant may be a small business's one and only budgeted consulting expense for the year, it may take longer to make the decision.

On the other hand, large businesses make numerous training and consulting purchases in a year. They may feel more comfortable taking a risk on a new consultant. Because this is not their one and only decision for the year, they can make hiring decisions faster. In addition, if you did a great job, you will have a better chance at repeat business with a larger organization. Small organizations may want to have you return, but may not have the budget.

---

*Go for the big fish;
you'll spend the same
time baiting the hook.*

Don't let the size of the organization scare you. The people who manage organizations need good consulting, no matter what the size. You will invest the same amount of time marketing your services to a large organization as to a small one. Your payoff, however, may be much greater.

Keep an Eye on Your Competition

One of the difficulties of being a consultant is being alone and outside the employment loop. Although it is psychologically difficult, it can be financially devastating if you do not keep up with what is going on in your field. What your competition does will affect your marketing plans.

Although you may have a specialty, be aware of the trends around you. How will a surge in downsizing affect what you provide? How will the latest management fad affect your philosophy? How will the changes in technology affect your service delivery?

Keep an eye on your competition. Read your professional journals: Who's advertising? What are they selling? Who's writing articles? Attend conferences: Who's presenting? What are they expounding? What's the buzz in the hallways? Visit bookstores: Who's writing? What topics are being published?

If you are not going to lead the profession, you must at the very least stay in touch. Your clients expect that of you.

Wallow in Your Junk Mail

Junk mail is a marketing research gift. Read it! You can spend thousands to find out what your competition is doing or you can acknowledge the free research delivered to your door every day. I often hear consultants complain about the piles of advertising they receive, especially in conjunction with conferences for which they have registered. Instead, welcome your junk mail as the gift it is.

What can you gain from your junk mail? You can develop a sense of the trends in the field. Trends are always changing. Is stress management "in" this year or "out"? Junk mail can spark ideas for your own marketing. Notice that I said spark ideas—not steal them. Junk mail can keep you informed of new people who have entered the field.

Don't bemoan your junk mail delivery. Instead, be grateful for all the competitive information that has just been dumped in your lap. Don't throw it away! Read it. Study it. Wallow in your junk mail!

Wallow in your junk mail!

Mail a Lumpy Envelope

The idea is to capture the recipient's attention so that the envelope is opened. You certainly don't want to think that your envelopes could be placed in someone's junk mail stack!

Over the years we have mailed dozens of lumpy envelopes. We've mailed typical things such as staple removers and holiday ornaments, but we've mailed the unusual, too, such as:

- Tree-shaped pasta in January to send greetings for a "tree-mendous" new year with many "pasta-bilities."
- Miniature books that contained quotes for business, for people, or for life.
- Tape measures asking the recipients how they measure up.
- Crayons to complete an interactive creativity brochure.
- Pumpkin pokes (black wire in the shape of bats that you "poke" into pumpkins) in October.

When there is nothing to make a large lump, we may add confetti to celebrate a business success or tiny stars to say congratulations. We have acquired a reputation for our lumpy envelopes. Some clients will only open our envelopes over a wastebasket. This marketing tactic has gained us a reputation for being creative and fun. In fact, deciding what the next lump could be is one of the most delightful things I do.

Mail a lumpy envelope.

Personalize Your Marketing

One of the rules of consulting states that a consultant should not be too close to the client because it prevents objectivity. I intentionally and completely ignore that rule. I want to get to know our clients as people and in doing so celebrate their humanness as well as their professionalism.

I do not do this as a marketing tactic. In fact, when I first started the business, most of my exchanges with clients were very informal and personal. I claimed that we did no marketing, until Ian, one of my clients, asked what I thought I was doing when I sent him a hand-made thank-you card? Whether it's marketing or not, I do believe it builds a strong relationship with my clients and potential clients.

How do we personalize marketing? We send cards filled with confetti to congratulate clients on job promotions. We send birthday cards. We send custom-designed cards to celebrate graduations, births, engagements, weddings, anniversaries, new cars, trips, a new life focus, a new house, a move. We send articles of interest about a favorite subject, hobby, child's college, vacation site, competitor, or mutual friend. We may send items that have a special meaning such as Georgia O'Keefe stamps, job ads, special coffee, music CDs, books (lots of books), pens, photos, good-luck tokens, or stones.

We send many notes to follow up on conversations. Sometimes items are added. I once had a conversation with a vice president of a large bank about the best training activity he ever saw: Analysis of the task of eating a piece of pie. Following that conversation, I sent him a piece of pie to tell him how much I enjoyed our conversation. Another time I had a discussion with a publisher in which we both marveled at the magic of television. I followed up by sending her a children's book, *How Things Work,* including the magic of television.

Remember that I do these things because I like people and I enjoy it! Although it may be seen as a marketing tool, I see it as a people tool. This will not work for everyone. I do it because it's who I am and I enjoy it. If it's not sincere, this kind of contact will backfire. If you are doing it "just to market your services," do not do it.

Know How to Acquire a New Client

Acquiring a new client requires ten times the effort as acquiring repeat business. I quoted Weinberg (1985), "The best way to get clients is to have clients," at the beginning of this chapter. This is true for two main reasons: First, if you are producing results, your clients will recommend you to other clients, and, second, if you are producing results, your clients will invite you back for additional projects.

---

*Acquiring a new client
requires ten times the effort
as acquiring repeat business.*

Many books written by successful consultants state that you will spend 25 to 40 percent of your time in marketing activities. I probably spent 80 percent of my time during the first months of start-up, but since then I have spent no more than 10 percent of my time marketing and most of that is of a very personal nature.

Use Your Clients to Market Your Services

The ideal situation for any consultant is to find that your clients speak highly of you and recommend you to other clients. Nothing, absolutely *nothing* is more valuable to you than a client's recommendation. You earn that by exceeding your customers' expectations, adding value at every point, producing the highest quality results, building trusting relationships, and modeling the highest ethics. In other words, doing a good job. Do good consulting!

Our vision statement says, "Our clients are so satisfied that they will market for us." Although it has taken a long time to achieve that vision, we have. We can trace more than 80 percent of our business back to three of our original clients.

113 TACTICS FOR LOW-BUDGET MARKETING

You need business. You need marketing tactics. You want to make a name for yourself, promote yourself, enhance your image, and build your reputation. But you have little money! What can you do? The following ideas will help you start. All will give you visibility and ensure that you stay in business. Some of these are common sense and you may already have thought of them. Others, on the other hand, may be too unusual for you. All of them should spark your creative thought process. All of them are tactics we have used.

1. Attend professional conferences to network.

2. Attend conferences for the industries that you serve.

3. Submit press releases to the media regarding your major consulting engagements, awards, published articles or books, or appointments.

4. Invite potential clients to a mini-presentation to get an idea of your expertise and services. Sometimes called showcases, these are often held in local hotels where food and beverages are served to encourage a more social atmosphere.

5. Find a reason to call special clients.

6. Become certified in your professional field to build credibility. Then announce it to your clients.

7. Join local civic organizations.

8. Join organizations that represent the industries you serve.

9. Join your professional organizations.

10. Attend local chapter meetings for the professional, civic, and social organizations to which you belong. Network! The greater the number of follow-up notes you write, the greater your success!

11. Plan to meet three new people in every networking situation.

12. Every time you meet a potential client, even a remotely potential client, follow up with a personal note.

13. Scan your newspaper for awards local business people have received and send a note congratulating them.

14. Speak at civic and professional organizations' meetings and conferences.

15. Identify and meet with people who can advance your career.

16. Take a client to lunch.

17. Meet with other consultants. If they are offered a project outside their scope of work, they may pass it on to you.

18. Bring the doughnuts if it's not in the client's budget.

19. When you are not given a project, send a thank you note saying you appreciated being considered. Compliment them on their choice—your competition.

20. Talk to a client about a new idea.

21. Send articles that will interest your present and potential clients.

22. Send a card for atypical holidays: Thanksgiving, Valentine's Day, St. Patrick's Day, Ground Hog Day, July Fourth.

23. Tie a client message to a holiday, for example, "We're thankful to have you as a client," "We're lucky to have you as a client," or "We have a reason to celebrate."

24. Send a lumpy envelope for a holiday: A gourd for Thanksgiving, candy hearts for Valentine's Day, a four-leaf clover for St. Patrick's Day, a sparkler for July Fourth.

25. Send birthday cards for both people and companies.

26. Send "congratulations" cards for promotions.

27. Send personal, hand-written thank you notes.

28. Listen to everything your clients are telling you. Find their needs.

29. Pass your extra work on to a trusted colleague. It will come back to you.

30. Help your client locate other consultants who can do work you are not qualified to do.

31. Share your expertise freely with clients and other consultants: Advice, ideas, materials, instruments. It will come back to you.

32. If you send brochures, announcements, or other information in the mail, add something unique, such as an oddly shaped envelope, a tube, or a colored envelope.

33. Send postcards when you're on vacation.

34. Page through a corporate specialty catalog to locate something around which you could build a theme. You will be surprised at some of the creative items you can purchase for under $2.00.

35. Visit a toy store looking for something around which you could build a marketing theme.

36. Send pictures of your support staff to your clients as a way to introduce the people who assist them by phone.

37. Support your local charity in the name of your clients. Send an announcement to your clients stating the details.

38. Sponsor a community event such as a 10K run.

39. Buy T-shirts for your employees, colleagues, or even clients.

40. Sponsor an offbeat memorable event. Perhaps you could rent your local theater for an afternoon and invite clients' children for a free showing.

41. Spread good rumors about your business, such as "We deliver high quality at a reasonable rate."

42. Invite an executive to breakfast.

43. Write letters to the editor of your newspaper or your professional journal.

44. Write newsworthy articles to publish in newspapers, for example, information about people in the industry, recent changes in an industry, or the "story behind the story" that made the headlines.

45. Write a column for your local newspaper. After the column is established, you can sell it to other newspapers.

46. Publish your own newsletter.

47. Write articles for your professional journal. Contact the editor to obtain a calendar of topics for the year.

48. Purchase professional-looking reprints of your article and send it to present and potential clients.

49. Write a book.

50. Send a copy of your book to present and potential clients.

51. Send any book your client would appreciate.

52. Invest in the best stationery and business cards you can afford.

53. If you are not ready to develop a brochure, create a fact sheet that concisely explains the benefits of your services.

54. Create a list of satisfied clients that you can share with potential clients.

55. Develop an autobiographical sketch that focuses on your strengths, lists some of your clients or the industries you work in, and identifies your accomplishments.

56. Post your business card or literature on public bulletin boards.

57. Ask your clients for referrals.

58. Give an award to one of your suppliers. This becomes a marketing tool for both of you.

59. Create a list of ten tips representing your specialty, such as "Ten tips for more efficient meetings," "Ten ways to reduce stress," or "Ten do's for financial planning." Print them on high quality paper with your name and telephone number. Mail them to clients or give them away at professional events.

60. Enter your projects in industry award competitions.

61. Collect testimonials.

62. Serve on a board for your community college, a local company, an association, or a charity.

63. Thank your clients—often.

64. Give something away free.

65. Refer new customers to your clients.

66. Provide new information to your clients on a regular basis.

67. Create your own mailing list. It should include everyone you meet in the line of business every day. We have a primary mailing list and a secondary mailing list. The primary list receives everything we send. The secondary list exists primarily for new product sales brochures. Your mailing list is a valuable marketing tool.

68. Offer a full money-back guarantee.

69. Trade show booths are generally very expensive, but you may be able to share one with another organization, or you could trade the cost of the booth for services to the association. Creativity, bed sheets, and lots of action can make up for the lack of the glitz and glamour of the more typical booths.

70. Create your own Website. However, if you do not have time to do it well and to keep it up to date, don't do it at all.

71. Purchase space in a directory or consultant database. Be sure to check on the rules. They may want a percent of each project you obtain from the listing.

72. Keep your key contacts alive. Plan how you will stay in touch with them, how often, and in what way.

73. When asked what you do, be prepared to further describe your consulting practice. Identify two or three quick examples to add more detail.

74. Love what you do. It will show.

75. Visit an industry trade show to compile a list of potential clients in an industry. You can visit their booths, speak with their employees, and pick up their literature.

76. Keep a supply of business cards with you. Hand them out freely everywhere you go.

77. Open a conversation with the person sitting next to you on the plane—especially if you are in first class.

78. Offer a finder's fee to colleagues who generate a project for you.

79. Prepare marketing around a theme, for example, send a ruler or tape measure asking potential clients how they measure up.

80. Find something that gives your correspondence a special touch. I've used round gold paper clips and small cards that have a special message sealed under a perforated flap.

81. Do things that make people feel special, such as using their names in the middle of the notes you write to them, sending pictures that you took at their team-building session, tracking down a special request they mentioned, or attributing an idea to them.

82. Respond to a Request for Proposals (RFP) from government agencies.

83. Check the *Commerce Business Daily,* a newspaper published by the U.S. government that lists opportunities to sell to the government. Many states also publish a similar document.

84. Following a presentation, have everyone toss a business card in a hat for a drawing. After drawing for the prizes, send a personal note to all who submitted a business card thanking the individuals for their attendance.

85. Contact your college roommate and ask for an introduction to an organization.

86. Donate a service or product to charity.

87. Stage a publicity stunt.

88. Agree to be interviewed on radio.

89. Conduct a survey. Publish the results. Share the results with clients.

90. Send samples of your materials or product to potential clients. For example, a computer software consultant could send a demo disk; a management consultant could send a self-evaluation.

91. Start all letters with "you" followed by a compliment.

92. Teach a class at a college or university.

93. Sponsor a round-table breakfast for members of a specific industry in one locale.

94. Volunteer your services to the media as a source of information about a specific industry. You will most likely be called for a quote.

95. Create a list of success stories you have had with past clients, such as an effort that resulted in a savings of $3 million each year and shortened the time from concept to catalog by eleven months.

96. Keep your travel expenses to a minimum. Your present clients will notice and appreciate it.

97. Call a former client if you plan to be visiting the city where the client is located.

98. Practice a perfect hand shake—not too firm, not too weak.

99. Create a key contact list. Update it and use it regularly.

100. Call future clients to request their quarterly reports. Use them to learn about the companies before visiting.

101. Purchase a focused mailing list from your professional association. Follow up the mailing with phone calls.

102. Purchase tapes of the speeches you give at conferences and send them to potential clients.

103. Write a letter to a television programming manager describing your idea for an appearance on television. Identify the connection to the show and the benefits to the viewers.

104. Start your own cable show.

105. Ask your neighbor for an introduction to an organization or individual.

106. Send geographic mailings before you visit a city. Send a note to several people letting them know you will be in their city. Follow up with a phone call to set a meeting time.

107. Make friends with secretaries and receptionists. All of them!

108. Host a summer picnic.

109. If you are a trainer, offer to conduct a pilot training program for a potential client for free.

110. Create a list of "client questions," questions you have used when meeting clients that have proven to be successful in getting to the heart of their problems.

111. Place ten cold calls.

112. Write a warm letter.

113. Most importantly, always give your client at least 113 percent of what they expected.

These 113 marketing tactics are just a start. You can think of others. The key is to find ways to promote who you are and what you do—and in the process to have fun!

POTENTIAL-CLIENT CONTACTS

Many people assume that contacting clients will be difficult and should therefore be avoided. It is easier than you might think.

Cold Calls

What is a person's greatest fear about making cold calls? Rejection. What can positively be guaranteed about making cold calls? Rejection. So create a positive cold-call attitude. I have a friend in sales who lives by cold calls. The numbers he works with are daunting. He says he must make one hundred cold calls to find ten people who will talk to him. Of those ten people, two will agree to meet with him and one will purchase his product.

So what if someone says "No," hangs up, or is rude? Don't let it bother you. You must refocus your attitude. You were not rejected; your services were rejected. The person did not need your services at this time. When you run into someone who frankly cannot use your services and he or she cuts the phone call short, you should *silently thank the person for not wasting your valuable time.* Rather than feeling rejected, you can feel thankful. Say "Thank you for your candor and have a great day!" Create your own cold call attitude.

Cold Call Warm-Ups

Quite honestly, I have made only a few cold calls in my life. I prefer to make warm calls. Although this takes more time, I believe I have better results and I enjoy the process more. To start, I warm up the client with a letter—not just any old letter, but one that I have written specifically for the client.

I begin by visiting the library to do research on a list of twenty to thirty potential clients with whom I'd like to do business. I use the library's resources, including local business magazines, journals and periodicals, local business newsletters, the newspaper, the city directory, manufacturer and business directories, and any other resources available. Each of these has an index that makes it easy to research the list of clients.

I use Exhibit 5.3, the company profile, to synthesize the information I find. If possible, I also copy articles that I find. I gather information for two key purposes: First, to learn as much as I can about the organization and, second, to have enough information to compose a unique letter that will grab the reader's attention. Examples of several of these letters are displayed in Exhibit 5.4.

Begin by making sure you are sending the letter to the right person. Double-check the spelling of the person's name and the person's title. Focus on the recipient in the first paragraph. Demonstrate that you know what is important to him or her. The second and third paragraphs should connect the recipient to the need for consulting services in some way and establish your qualifications. Both of these paragraphs must be customized. For example, when referring to past clients, select only those who are related to the recipient by industry, location, or size. If that is not possible, select only a couple of your most impressive clients. In the last paragraph tell the recipient what to expect next. I developed this format twenty years ago and continue to obtain remarkable results.

I usually find information for 30 to 50 percent of the clients on the list that I take to the library. After I return to the office, I compose the letters and mail them. I follow the letter with a telephone call on the date that is stated in the letter.

Ninety-five percent of all recipients are interested in speaking with me, and more than half of them agree to a meeting within a month. Of those, about half

💾 Exhibit 5.3. Company Profile.

Name _____

Address _____

_____

Telephone _____ Employees _____

Management Positions

_____   _____

_____   _____

_____   _____

_____   _____

_____   _____

Products _____

History _____

_____

_____

Financial Information _____

Philosophy _____

_____

Training Design _____

Additional Relevant Information _____

_____

Resources _____

▣ Exhibit 5.4a. Sample Introductory Marketing Letter.

July 12, 20XX

Robert R. Birkhauser, President
Auto Glass Specialists, Inc.
2810 Syene Road
Madison, WI 53713

Dear Mr. Birkhauser:

Auto Glass Specialists is one of Madison's phenomenons. In just over twenty years you have transformed an innovative idea into a successful business spanning five states. Your expertise for repairing windows in cars, trucks, and heavy equipment is now available in twenty-three locations, with sales pushing $15 million. Strong management and hard-working employees achieved these results.

At ebb associates we recognize the important role the employee plays in the successful growth of any company. Further, we have found that improving employees' communication skills results in improved productivity and increased profit. Do you realize that just one one-hundred-dollar listening mistake by each of Auto Glass Specialists' two hundred employees can result in a loss of $20,000 each year? Improved communication skills can decrease mistakes, increase your profits, and improve customer relations.

ebb associates specializes in communication training. We present workshops and seminars focusing on improved communication and will custom-design a program to meet your needs at Auto Glass Specialists. Our clients, including Tenneco Automotive and Cardinal Glass, recognize our commitment to meeting their needs, providing excellent follow-up, and obtaining results. We'd like to help you, too, so that you can improve the quality and increase the quantity of work by maximizing the potential of your human resources.

I would like to call you within the week to schedule an appointment to discuss how we can assist you to meet your goals at Auto Glass Specialists. I am enclosing a list of the course titles that we can customize to meet your specific needs. I look forward to meeting and working with you.

Sincerely,

Elaine Biech
ebb associates

⊞ Exhibit 5.4b. Sample Introductory Marketing Letter.

July 12, 20XX

Roger Brown, President
Rocky Rococo Corporation
First Gilman Corporation
333 West Mifflin Street
Madison, WI 53703

Dear Mr. Brown:

From Brown's Diner to fifteen units and franchising plans is a success story that could only be written by the best Chicago pan-style pizza. This exceptional product is a result of your high standards for consistency and quality. In addition, we know that Rocky Rococo values people highly. You do not want customers to wait too long; yet you want them to experience the best pan-style pizza in the nation. You offer variety yet consistency—thus your unique system of selling pizza by the slice. You want families to feel at home—thus your new Hostess Program.

We at ebb associates value people, too. In fact, staying in touch with the needs of a company and its employees is our specialty. We work with companies that are interested in improving their productivity through improved communication. Managers and supervisors who participate in our training programs have found that, as their communication and management skills improve, so do the quality and quantity of work. ebb associates presents workshops and seminars on supervisory training, management development, sales training, and customer relations. Our clients, including Land O' Lakes, Dorman-Roth Foods, Hershey Chocolate, and many others, recognize our commitment to meeting their needs, providing exceptional training, and obtaining results.

Opening eight new stores in the next year in such places as Oshkosh, La Crosse, and Milwaukee will not be an easy task. We at ebb associates would like to show you how improved communication can result in a smoother expansion plan, reduce mistakes, and continue to improve customer relations.

I will call you within the week to schedule an appointment to discuss how we can assist you to meet your goals at Rocky Rococo. I am enclosing a list of the course titles that we will customize for your specific needs.

Sincerely,

Elaine Biech
ebb associates

🖫 Exhibit 5.4c. Sample Introductory Marketing Letter.

July 12, 20XX

Terry Voice, President
Pizza Pit Ltd.
2154 Atwood Avenue
Madison, WI 53704

Dear Mr. Voice:

Free, fast, hot delivery has placed Pizza Pit a step ahead of the rest. In fourteen years you have turned this unique idea into a successful business with over $6 million in sales. Pizza Pit has grown from one location to a chain of nine Dane County stores with franchising plans on the board. Two hundred franchised units in five years is an ambitious goal—one we're sure you will achieve!

At ebb associates we recognize the important role employees play in the successful growth of any company. Further, we have found that improving employees' communication skills results in improved productivity and increased profit. Your anticipated rate of growth will require you to be on top of the communication needs of your staff for a smoother expansion.

ebb associates presents workshops and seminars that focus on communication for supervisory training, management development, sales training, and customer relations. Our clients, including Land O' Lakes, McDonald's Corporation, and many others, recognize us for our commitment to excellence in training, customizing to fit individual company needs, and obtaining results.

Enclosed is a list of the course titles that we will customize to meet your needs. I will call you within the week to schedule an appointment to discuss how we can assist you to meet your expansion goals at Pizza Pit. I promise a free, fast, hot delivery!

Sincerely,

Elaine Biech
ebb associates

💾 Exhibit 5.4d. Sample Introductory Marketing Letter.

July 12, 20XX

Fred Huber, President
Jos. Huber Brewing Company
1208 Fourteenth Avenue
Monroe, WI 53566

Dear Mr. Huber:

Producing a high quality product is of utmost importance to you and your staff at the Jos. Huber Brewing Company. You have achieved that goal by receiving *The Great American Beer Book*'s number one rating of Augsburger. Congratulations! I'm sure you strive for that same quality in each of the sixteen brands of beer produced under your brewmaster's care.

We at ebb associates strive for a quality product, too: a number-one rating. ebb associates specializes in communication training. We present workshops and seminars focusing on improving communication in connection with supervisory training, management development, and sales training. Our clients report that improving employees' communication skills results in improved productivity and increased profit. We work with many Wisconsin companies such as the Kohler Company, S.C. Johnson and Son, and Lands' End that are interested in results. These companies recognize our ability to provide excellent training by customizing to meet their needs.

I'd like an opportunity to show you how you can squeeze more profits out of the half-million barrels of the fine beer you produce each year. I will call you within the week to schedule an appointment to discuss how we can assist you to meet your future goals at the Jos. Huber Brewing Company. I am enclosing a list of the course titles that we will customize for your specific needs. I look forward to meeting and working with you.

Sincerely,

Elaine Biech
ebb associates

⊟ Exhibit 5.4e. Sample Introductory Marketing Letter.

July 12, 20XX

Richard E. McElvain, Vice President
Warmen International, Inc.
2701 South Stoughton Road
Madison, WI 53716

Dear Mr. McElvain:

Madison is an unusual location for a manufacturer of centrifugal slurry pumps
used in mining. That was my initial reaction. On second thought, however,
I realized that Madison is very centrally located to everyone with whom you
work: the iron mines in Minnesota, the copper mines in Utah and Nevada, the
coal mines in West Virginia, and the foundries here in Wisconsin. This central
location has certainly contributed to your rapid expansion. You have risen from
not being in the U.S. market at all prior to coming to Madison in 1971 to sales of
$21 million last year. Expansion is probably in your future plans also.

We at ebb associates recognize the importance of communication to successfully
fulfilling goals. ebb associates presents workshops and seminars that focus on
improved communication. We work with companies such as Sperry Marine,
Diebold, Newport News Shipbuilding, and many others who are interested in
improving their productivity through improved communication. We recognize
that the economy has not been kind to companies directly related to the mining
industry. However, our clients agree that productivity and profits can be increased
through improved communication while we await the economy's turnaround.

You feel that your equipment is "the best investment a buyer can make." We look
at our communication training as an excellent investment a company can make.
I will call you within the week to schedule an appointment to discuss how we
can assist you to meet your goals at Warmen International. What kind of an
investment can we help you make?

Sincerely,

Elaine Biech
ebb associates

🖫 Exhibit 5.4f. Sample Introductory Marketing Letter.

July 12, 20XX

Albert H. Felly, President
Felly's Flowers
205 E. Broadway Street
Madison, WI 53716

Dear Mr. Felly:

We know that you at Felly's Flowers take pride in the individual care you give each of the plants you grow. You water almost all of the six hundred species of plants by hand to insure that they grow and flourish. You have an automatic fertilizing system, but again, acids and fertilizers are provided only if needed. We recognize that Felly's reputation for high quality plants and flowers can be attributed to the individual attention you provide for each.

Just as you are an expert at growing flowers, we at ebb associates specialize in communication training. We recognize that individual care must be given to employees if a company is to grow and flourish. Did you know that 50 percent of all mistakes in the business world are made due to misunderstanding, not lack of skills or job knowledge? Therefore, improving employees' communication skills is vital to the success of any business.

ebb associates presents workshops and seminars that focus on improved communication. We work with companies, such as Famous Fixtures, General Casualty Company, James River Corporation, and many others, that are interested in improving their productivity through improved communication. These companies recognize our ability to meet their needs, provide excellent follow-up, and obtain measurable results. We'd like to provide training for the Felly's staff so that you, too, can decrease mistakes, increase profits, and improve customer relations.

Improving employees' communication skills is one of the ways to fertilize the desired growth of a company. I would like to call you within the week to schedule an appointment to discuss how we can assist you to meet your goals at Felly's Flowers. I am enclosing a list of the course titles that we can customize for your specific needs and look forward to meeting and working with you.

Sincerely,

Elaine Biech
ebb associates

become clients in less than one year. The rest become contacts, resources, or clients in the future. These odds are much better than for cold calls, and the process is more fun. I enjoy the challenge of the research and the creativity of the letter composition. I particularly like beginning a relationship in this positive way.

Exhibit 5.5 provides a list of questions to ask potential clients. You can use these to guide your discussions on the telephone or in person.

Exhibit 5.5. Questions to Ask Potential Clients.

1. What does your company (division, department) value most?
2. What are your company's (division's, department's) vision and mission?
3. What is your strategy to achieve your vision and mission?
4. What are your company's (division's, department's, leadership team's) strengths?
5. What's going well for your company (division, department, team)?
6. What are the greatest challenges you will face over the next two years?
7. What prevents you from achieving your goals (objectives, mission)?
8. What do you see as the greatest need for improvement?
9. What prevents you from making that improvement?
10. Describe the communication process in your company (division, department). How well does it work?
11. If you had one message to give your company president (CEO, board of directors, manager), what would it be?
12. What should I have asked, but did not?

Ways to Track Client Contacts

After you begin to contact clients, you will want to track who you called when, what they said, what you sent them, and when they have asked you to call again. Exhibit 5.6 will help you keep this information organized.

🔲 Exhibit 5.6. Client Contact Log.

Organization/ Phone Number	Contact Person	Date	First Contact	FU*	Date	Second Contact	FU	Date	Third Contact	FU

*FU = Follow-Up

Questions Clients Will Ask

Clients who have used consultants in the past will ask many of the same questions. Most will want to know what you do. Know how to tell your story in a sixty-second sound bite. I experience the following variations repeatedly.

---

*Know how to tell your story
in a sixty-second sound bite.*

- What are the deliverables? What will the final product look like?
- What are the critical milestones? At what point will progress, quality, quantity be checked? How?
- How much will this cost me? (Answer this one using the word "investment," for example, "Your investment for completing this project will be $13,900.")
- What are your billing practices? How often will you invoice me?
- How can you help me with the kick-off of this project?
- Whom do I contact if there are problems or concerns?
- How can we stay in contact?
- How can you help me communicate with my boss?
- What is our responsibility at each phase? How will you involve our employees?
- How will you evaluate the success of this project?

If Your Clients Don't Ask

What if the client does not ask questions? Perhaps your client has little experience working with consultants. You will still want to ensure that certain basics have been covered in your discussion. If your client does not ask, introduce the topic by saying, "You probably want to know. . . ." This puts the topic on the table in an efficient way. The list of questions in Exhibit 5.5 can be adapted for this purpose.

If you have read Peter Block's (1981) *Flawless Consulting* (and you should have if you are considering a consulting career), you undoubtedly recognize that you are moving into the contracting phase of the consulting process. Contracting is ensuring that both you and your client are as explicit as possible about your needs, wants, and expectations of one another. Contracting is covered more completely in Chapter Seven. The contracting discussion is an important link to writing a good proposal.

PROPOSALS AND CONTRACTS

Proposals and contracts are two written documents that you will probably use at some point in your career. Each serves a purpose for staying in business.

Proposals

I use proposals frequently and like them. Often I am asked to submit a proposal as a step in competing for a project. At other times I am asked to submit a proposal to clarify a previous discussion. The proposal will identify *who* will do *what* by *when* and for *how much*. I actually like to write proposals. It clarifies the project in my mind, and I find myself developing creative possibilities during the process.

A proposal typically includes a purpose statement; a description of the situation as it now exists; a proposed approach that the consultant will take (this may include data gathering, design of materials, content relationships, delivery of services, and implementation); a timeline; the consultant's qualifications; and the investment required to complete the plan.

I guarantee that you will write the best proposal if you listen to what your client says and take good notes. Do not take this statement lightly. In fact, reread it. Take it in. After reading our proposals, clients often say complimentary things about the proposal, such as, "This is exactly what we need! How did you know?" We knew because we listened and we fed back their exact words. Consultants make a big mistake by putting things in their own words. If the client has requested an attitude survey, identify it that way in your proposal. An "employee satisfaction survey" may be more meaningful to you and the resulting surveys may have the identical words on paper. Unfortunately, your client will not know that.

———————

*You will write the best proposal
if you listen to what your client says
and take good notes.*

———————

Specify an effective date, for example, "The terms of this proposal are effective through April 30, 1999." You do not want to get caught by a client who has a proposal that is two years old and for which the budget was just approved. Why is this a problem? First, the fee you quoted may be lower than what you presently charge. In addition, you have most likely grown and improved your skills, so the process you have proposed may be outdated. Finally, an effective date reduces the amount of time a client will keep you dangling.

We like to use the word "investment" (as opposed to cost or price) when we write proposals. It echoes our philosophy that we believe what we do adds value and that it does not just cost money.

Proposals are often written in competition with other consultants. They may range in length from one to fifty pages. A one-page proposal may be considered a letter of agreement. An informed client will be as interested in the content of the proposal as in the price. Exhibit 5.7 provides an example of a proposal.

Contracts

Contracts are legal documents that bind both parties to the content stated. I personally do not like them because I believe they start the relationship on a trust-questioning level. Contracts usually involve the legal department, which usually holds the project up for a time. Except for our government work, most of our work is conducted on the basis of a clarifying proposal or a handshake.

What should contracts look like? What should they say? No matter how complete we have been or what we have written in contracts, legal departments have always slashed them apart. I recommend that you have the client's legal department initiate the contract. It will save you a great deal of time and frustration. If you believe a contract will provide you with security or clarity, use it. Quite honestly, I believe a well-written proposal meets our needs better. We use contracts when it makes the client feel more comfortable with the new relationship.

Contracts frequently include terms (effective dates), project scope, deliverables, confidentiality, communication, staffing, supervision of the consultant, scheduling, payment schedule, incentives and penalties, termination terms, the cancellation policy, arbitration arrangements, transfer of responsibilities, taxes, and modifications to the contract. Exhibit 5.8 provides a simple version of a contract drawn up by a client.

💾 Exhibit 5.7. Sample Proposal.

Progressive Discipline:
Consistency Is the Key

Purpose

This proposal is submitted at the request of Jack Smith, Vice President of Human Resources, National Underwriters. It includes the situation, a suggested approach, timeline, and expected investment for the effort.

The Situation

The goal of National Underwriters' progressive discipline training is to ensure that progressive discipline is handled consistently across the company. To ensure that this occurs, supervisors must be able to:

- Identify employee behaviors that must be changed, based on National Underwriters' performance and policy standards.
- Define and implement the progressive discipline process consistently.
- Document in detail the steps to be taken.

This session will ensure that supervisors leave with a clear understanding of how to ensure consistency.

In addition to ensuring consistency, supervisors will also be able to:

- Understand the cost to the company of inconsistency.
- Define the progressive discipline regulations for the state in which each supervisor works.
- Identify the legal ramifications of inconsistent actions.
- Review the policy statement and locate it within the employee handbook.
- Clarify the concept of "fair dealing."
- Identify skills necessary to decrease the number and intensity of difficult disciplinary situations.
- Make consistent decisions when presented with an unclear situation.
- Discuss the importance of consistent progressive discipline in relation to the statements "The Client Comes First" and "People Make the Difference."

🖫 Exhibit 5.7. Sample Proposal, Cont'd.

Supervisors will become experts to ensure consistent treatment of every employee in the organization. To ensure this, we will custom design a session using your examples, your language, your progressive disciplinary process, and your standards of conduct. Your unique needs will be addressed.

Proposed Approach

Information and Data Gathering. To design a relevant training session for you, data gathering is required. To accomplish this we will do the following:

- Interview Jack Smith, vice president, and Donna Dopp, corporate attorney, to determine their desired objectives for this session.
- Interview National Underwriters' attorneys for examples of past lessons learned.
- Interview HR and line managers who have experienced the progressive discipline process.
- Review job descriptions, training curriculum, employee-orientation materials, and other documentation that defines expected supervisory performance.
- Request a list of supervisors and their experience, including tenure, training, and previous relevant work experience.
- Review your vision and strategy statements for the next five years, historical information, names and positions of key people in the organization, a listing of jargon and acronyms we may need to know, and other documentation you deem appropriate.

Custom Design. Your materials will be custom designed for the organization, making it much easier for supervisors to accept, learn, and implement.

Our data gathering will provide examples that we will build into the training design, corporate jargon we will learn and use, strategies to ensure that the training "sticks," and actual situations that we will develop into role plays, case studies, and other hands-on activities.

In addition, the design will ensure that critical factors of adult learning theory are built into the session. The training will do the following:

💾 Exhibit 5.7. Sample Proposal, Cont'd.

- Build on the knowledge and concepts the participants already possess.
- Use actual corporate examples.
- Relate the learning to the needs of each participant.
- Allow opportunity for interaction and questions.
- Provide hands-on skill practice.
- Build in mechanisms for participant feedback.
- Present a plan for immediate action and feedback.
- Provide a job aid for supervisors to ensure consistency of the process.

Content. Final content will be determined as a result of the data-gathering process. The session will ensure that participants achieve all objectives identified in the first section of this proposal. Final content will be determined at a meeting scheduled for March 14, 2000.

All of the content will be directly related to National Underwriters. Examples will be based on four areas within the company:

- Software development
- Data centers—account processing
- Item or check processing
- Small manufacturing/software companies.

Materials. National Underwriters will be given an exclusive copyright for all participant materials designed for this project.

Conducting the Course. We believe this course will require one day's training, allowing supervisors to return to their offices at the end of the day. We recommend that a maximum of eighteen participants attend. If that number increases, it will be necessary to increase the session time.

Implementation. At your request, a pilot session will be held on May 16, 2000, in Troy, Michigan. Your staff will conduct the session and six to eighteen of your first-line supervisors/managers will participate to ensure that we have perfected the materials before they are presented to the rest of the organization. The pilot is also important to ensure that the timing is adequate for your employees.

📄 Exhibit 5.7. Sample Proposal, Cont'd.

We will observe this session to provide feedback to your trainers, to ensure that the materials meet your unique needs, to answer any implementation questions, and to determine whether changes need to be made.

In addition, we will facilitate an evaluation following the pilot session in which participants will be asked to provide answers to the following questions:

- What should be emphasized more? Less?
- Do we need to increase the time spent in any area? Decrease time spent in any area?
- Is there too much material for the time available and, if so, what should be cut? Should additional training hours be added? How else can this information be learned?
- Have we missed anything? What should be added?
- What errors must be corrected?

This evaluation process serves to guarantee our work. Any changes or corrections will be provided without additional charge.

Follow Up. A critical but often overlooked step in the training process is the follow up to reinforce the skills. We will provide ideas that will be initiated by your training staff and the supervisors. These could include suggestions such as:

- A "rap" session open to anyone in supervisory positions to ensure continued growth, answer concerns or questions, and to enhance teamwork among supervisors.
- Peer mentoring.
- A reading list.
- A "lessons learned" board.
- A refresher session.

Timeline

March 14, 2000	Decision on final course objectives
March 22, 2000	Interviews and data gathering begin
April 4, 2000	Design begins
April 18, 2000	First draft available for National Underwriters
May 9, 2000	Final approval by National Underwriters
May 16, 2000	Pilot

Exhibit 5.7. Sample Proposal, Cont'd.

We can begin the data-gathering stage by mid-March and have the design completed by mid-May. Other dates can be finalized on acceptance of this proposal.

Investment and Responsibilities

We would like to have one contact person within the company who is knowledgeable about the project and who understands the goals. This individual will assist us with scheduling interviews, distributing information, and answering our questions.

The investment includes the design and delivery of all aspects of the effort outlined in this proposal, including, but not limited to:

- All planning and coordination
- All data and information gathering and compilation
- All interview preparation, coordination, and facilitation
- A one-day session titled "Progressive Discipline: Consistency Is the Key"
- A pilot session on May 16, 2000
- A training guide for HR trainers
- Participant materials for the pilot session
- Audiovisual materials for the pilot session
- A master of "Progressive Discipline: Consistency Is the Key" participant materials
- A master of overhead transparencies
- An exclusive copyright for all participant materials designed for this project

Your investment for course design, pilot observation, and exclusive copyright is $12,900. In addition, travel will be billed at cost.

The terms of this proposal are effective through June 30, 2000.

Executive-level and/or expert trainer references are available.

💾 Exhibit 5.8. Sample Contract.

Agreement

Agreement made and entered into this 3rd day of January 2000, by and between
_____ (client) of _____(address)_____ (hereinafter "Purchaser")
and consultant of _____(address)_____ (hereinafter "Consultant").

In consideration of the mutual covenants and promises contained herein, and for good and valuable consideration, the parties hereby agree as follows:

I. Project Responsibilities and Obligations

Consultant will develop and implement a Member Service Staff Training and Intervention plan as further detailed in Exhibit A to this contract, which is hereby incorporated by reference. Implementation of said plan will be based on input and guidelines provided by Purchaser. Implementation of said plan will include, but will not necessarily be limited to, the following components:

A. Gathering Information and Data;

B. Designing Three Training Courses;

C. Conducting Training Courses;

D. Designing Training Materials; and

E. Providing Consultation Services.

These are detailed further in Exhibit A herein. Delivery of services shall reasonably conform to the timeline set forth in Exhibit B.

Responsibilities for each party shall be as follows:

Purchaser

1. Provide one contact person who is knowledgeable about the project and who understands the goals of this effort. This individual will assist with establishing meetings, scheduling interviews, copying and distributing information, and completing other coordination tasks.

2. Provide copies of the participant materials for the last four sessions of Member Services Staff Training.

3. Provide training space and all audiovisual equipment for the training sessions, including an overhead projector and two flip charts for each session. A video camera, monitor, and tape deck will also be required for the two-day Train-the-Trainer session.

📎 Exhibit 5.8. Sample Contract, Cont'd.

Consultant

1. Complete all aspects required to implement the plan outlined above, including, but not limited to:

   - All planning and coordination
   - All data and information gathering and compilation
   - All interview preparation, coordination, and facilitation
   - Design of a one-day session titled Member Services Staff Training
   - Design of a two-day Train-the-Trainer session for six to ten individuals
   - Design of a one-day Coaching session for supervisors
   - Training materials for Member Services and Coaching sessions
   - A training guide and outline for the Train-the-Trainer session
   - Participant materials for the pilot of the Member Services session, the Train-the-Trainer session, and the Coaching session
   - All audiovisual materials

2. Provide materials ensuring the Purchaser's self-sufficiency following the implementation, including but not limited to:

   - Master of Member Services Staff Training participant materials
   - Master of Member Services Staff Training overhead transparencies

3. Provide an agreement following the final follow-up on-site visit that outlines arrangements for shared copyright for all participant materials designed for this project. The agreement will state that the materials shall be used by the Purchaser for internal use only. The materials may not be sold. The materials may be used externally with written permission from Consultant.

4. Invoice monthly for work completed plus travel expenses.

II. Consideration

In exchange for Consultant's services, as set forth in Section I above, Purchaser will pay Consultant monthly, total compensation not to exceed thirty-eight thousand two hundred dollars ($38,200). Consultant will be paid as services are rendered in any given month as set forth above, excluding 5 percent ($1,910), which will be held until completion of the full engagement. Final payment will be made within thirty days of receipt of a bill itemizing charges incurred to complete all services.

III. Travel Expenses

In addition to the consideration set forth in Section II above, Purchaser will pay to Consultant reasonable and necessary expenses as specifically set forth herein. Reimbursement of expense shall include charges incurred for travel (airfare, mileage, car rental and/or train fare), lodging, and meals during trips to the Purchaser's site. All travel expenses shall be procured at the lowest cost available. Travel dates are outlined in Exhibit B.

Reimbursement for travel expenses shall be paid within thirty days from invoice date by Purchaser on submission of receipts, evidencing out-of-pocket expenses incurred by Consultant.

IV. Term

This agreement will take effect as of the date indicated in the introductory paragraph above and shall extend until Consultant's completion of all services set forth in Section I unless earlier termination by the Purchaser on the giving of written notice. On any such notice of termination, services by Consultant shall be discontinued and compensation will cease to accrue.

V. Confidential Information

A. On being notified that a party to this Agreement considers information confidential, each party hereto agrees not to disclose the confidential information of the other party, directly or indirectly, under any circumstances or by any means, to any third person, without express, written consent obtained in advance. Each party hereto agrees that it will not copy, transmit, reproduce, summarize, quote, or make any commercial or other use whatsoever of the other party's confidential information, except as provided herein. Each party agrees to exercise the highest degree of care in safeguarding the confidential information of the other party against loss, theft, or inadvertent disclosure and agrees generally to take all steps necessary to ensure the maintenance of confidentiality.

B. On termination of this agreement or as otherwise requested, each party agrees to deliver promptly to the other party all confidential information of that party, in whatever form, that may be in its possession or under its control.

VI. No Transfer

This Agreement shall not be assigned or transferred by either party without the express written consent of the other party, obtained in advance.

VII. Taxes

Both parties shall promptly pay all applicable taxes of every kind, nature, and description arising out of the establishment, nature, and operation of its business in connection with the event described in this Agreement.

VIII. Notices

All notices to be given and communications in connection with this Agreement shall be in writing and addressed to the parties at the following addresses:

Consultant	Purchaser
_____	_____
(Consultant)	(Client)
(address)	(address)
(address)	(address)

IX. Effect of Partial Invalidity

The invalidity of any portion of this Agreement will not and shall not be deemed to affect the validity of any other provision. In the event that any provision of this Agreement is held to be invalid, the parties agree that the remaining provisions shall be deemed to be in full force and effect as if they had been executed by both parties subsequent to the expurgation of the invalid provision.

X. Modification of Agreement

Any modification of this Agreement or additional obligations assumed by either party in connection with this Agreement shall be binding only if placed in writing and signed by each party or an authorized representative of each party.

By the Parties:

_____   _____
Name, Title   Name, Title
(Client)   (Consultant)

_____   _____
Date   Date

HOW TO REFUSE AN ASSIGNMENT

There will be times when it is better to walk away from an assignment than to accept it. I was once called to conduct a team building for a manager for whom I had completed some previous work. During our second planning discussion, he began to make some unusual requests—all directed toward one employee. It turned out that he really was not looking for a team-building session, but for evidence and documentation that could be used to fire someone on his staff! Needless to say, I turned the job down.

In another situation, our firm was selected based on our proposal and interviews to coordinate a major change effort that would occur over an eighteen-month time frame. One of our contingencies was a satisfactory meeting with the CEO. When I met with him, I found that he supported the change for all the wrong reasons and that it was unlikely that his support would continue when the going got tough. I ended our conversation with, "It doesn't seem that you are ready for this change. We will be unable to accept this challenge until you can guarantee your full support." There was a lot of sputtering and disbelief. He had never heard of a consultant turning down work. I left saying that if he wanted me to help him prepare for what was ahead I would do so, but otherwise we would not accept the project. He called that same afternoon and I spent several sessions with him explaining exactly what he was getting himself into.

Yes, there are times when you will refuse an assignment, including some of the following:

- The client asks you to do something unethical or clandestine or you just feel uncomfortable about the project.
- The project lacks support from the right levels of management.
- The project is doomed for failure. It is unethical to take the client's money in that situation.
- The scope is too large for the money available.
- The project requires a steep learning curve for you, but the time is not available for the learning to occur.
- You do not have the time to do the project with your usual high quality.
- The chemistry is missing between you and the client.

WAYS TO STAY IN BUSINESS

Many things can happen to ensure that you stay in business. Only one thing will ensure that you go out of business—a lack of work. Staying in business is dependent on a steady flow of clients. Put your marketing plan together and then do it! You will starve waiting for the phone to ring!

The Cost of Doing Business

"Error is only the opportunity to begin again, more intelligently."

Henry Ford

Even if your business is up and running quickly, you land a couple of big contracts, and you have satisfied customers, you must study the numbers to know whether you are financially successful. Study your numbers? Here's what you are looking for.

- *Cash Flow.* Will you have enough money to pay your bills this month?
- *Expenses.* Where is all the money going? Which expenses are constant (those that do not change when business increases or decreases, such as rent, salaries, and insurance)? Which expenses vary depending on the level of business, such as travel, printing and professional fees?
- *Overhead.* What does it take to keep your business open?
- *Profitability.* Which contracts are the most lucrative?
- *Capital.* What business expenses are good investments?
- *Invoices.* How readily are they being paid?

This chapter will help you examine various aspects of recording, tracking, and reading your numbers. It will also provide suggestions to improve your financial picture. Forms are also provided that will save you weeks of work. The advice in this chapter can prevent dozens of mistakes.

PLAN FOR THE WORST

To keep myself out of financial trouble I follow this advice: Plan for the worst-case scenario, but act as if you're living the best case. There are two messages inherent in this statement: First, *don't spend your money until it's in your hands.* One of your clients may not pay you on time; the loan you were counting on may not be approved; an unexpected expense may occur, such as replacing your fax machine.

---

*Plan for the worst-case scenario,
but act as if you're living the best case.*

The first message is practical, but the second message is philosophical. "Act as if you're living the best case" refers to the message you are sending to yourself and others. As a strong believer in positive thinking, I am convinced that much of my company's success is due to the fact that I expect it. I believe I will succeed. You must also *live the best case for your clients.* Never hint to a client that business is less than great. Suggesting that your business is having financial difficulty will make clients nervous about your stability and even wary about your ability to perform the job. I've noticed that even the smallest complaint, such as "Our paper wasn't delivered on time," can cause concern. So do not mention your problems to your clients. You want confidence, not sympathy.

Whenever you play with your numbers, remind yourself to "Plan for the worst-case scenario, but act as if you're living the best case." Most consultants do exactly the opposite.

Plan for problems. Portray prosperity.

WATCH YOUR CASH FLOW

You can be very profitable and still go out of business. A surprising statement? Yes, but true. Your books can display a 20 percent profit on every project, but if cash flowing into your business does not meet cash flowing out, you will find yourself in a very difficult situation. Cash-flow problems are the number one reason that small businesses fail. You can control cash flow. Try some or all of these suggestions to prevent cash-flow problems.

*Do not mention your
problems to your clients.*

Bill Immediately

Make billing for work you have completed your number two priority. (Meeting customers' needs should always be your first priority.) Complete and mail your clients' invoices as soon as you finish the work. The same day is not too soon. Many organizations, including federal government agencies, have a thirty-day time frame from the date they receive the invoice to the day they cut the check. If you wait a week or two to send the bill, it could be a full sixty days before you receive cash for the work you completed. Remember, they cannot pay you if you don't bill them!

Billing immediately is important for reasons beyond preventing cash-flow problems. The sooner you bill, the more pleased the client will be about paying immediately. Unfortunately, the value of your services diminishes with time. A client may begin to think that what you accomplished was actually a very small aspect of the total success of the project or even that the solution was his or her own, not yours! The lesson? Bill while the client is most satisfied with your work.

*You can be very profitable
and still go out of business.*

Use a Reliable Delivery System to Send Invoices

Ensure that your client receives your invoice. Send your invoices in a priority mail packet. The cost will be $3.00 or more, as opposed to $.32, but the United States Postal Service will give this mail better attention. Your invoice will have a better chance of reaching its destination in a shorter amount of time. We could give many examples of delayed or lost mail. In general, first class mail between our Virginia and Wisconsin offices takes five to ten days. Some routine mail takes over four weeks! The priority mail packets usually arrive in fewer than five days. In addition, your client may give it special attention due to the packaging. If the invoice is a large amount or you need to have it turned around quickly, skip the U. S. Postal Service entirely and send your invoice in a letter packet with your favorite private carrier.

Monitor Accounts Receivable Methodically

At the end of every week, the bookkeeper on staff provides me with a cash-flow report. It identifies the amount in our checking and savings accounts, overdue invoices, and those due this month and next. The report also highlights significant expenses, such as noting that payroll will be taken out the following week.

Know Your Clients' Reputation for Prompt Payment

The strategy you have chosen will often define how readily your clients pay you. Most clients I work with pay within our thirty-day expectations. Some industries are notoriously late; some of your clients may be late on occasion.

For example, if you have decided that providing service to the federal government is your niche, find out what you are getting into. First, while there is a prompt payment law, some agencies have a difficult time paying within thirty days. This is not due to a lack of funds, but to a lack of efficient processes. As I write this, one of our organizations is five months behind in paying us due to some technicality. We know we will be paid, but we do not know when! This can be detrimental to your cash flow if you are not prepared for it. Second, government work is fickle. Here today, gone tomorrow. Even with a contract signed, the federal government has the right to cancel at any time. As a taxpayer, I am fine with that. I don't want my tax dollars spent if they should not be spent.

Government work is fickle.

Serving government agencies, especially our Department of Defense clients, has always been a rewarding part of our work, so we don't want to eliminate it. Our strategy is to have government contracts generate a maximum of 20 percent of our revenue. This strategy has helped us balance working with great clients and maintaining a healthy revenue stream for the business.

Include Project Initiation Fees in Your Proposals

You can prevent cash-flow concerns by requesting a sum in advance to initiate the contract. Put an amount in your proposal, normally a few thousand dollars to cover initial out-of-pocket expenses such as travel. Your contract could read, "$3,000 is due to initiate this project and to cover initial out-of-pocket expenses." We prefer to avoid this technique, because we want to always project an image of success—including financial success. The technique, while perfectly legitimate and used by many successful firms to show commitment from the client, can suggest a shortage of cash.

*They cannot pay you
if you don't bill them!*

Offer a Prepayment Discount

Some consultants offer their clients a discount of 3 to 7 percent if they prepay. I have never done this, but those who use it like it. I admit that the reason I do not use this technique is that it feels amateurish. Others offer a 1 to 3 percent discount for early payment, say within ten days of the invoice date.

Refrain from Paying Client Expenses

Rather than paying for copying, research, or other direct client costs out of your pocket, send the invoices to the client. Paying for them yourself and then asking for reimbursement can tie up your cash for over thirty days.

Make Your Money Work for You

Cash-flow problems can be reduced if you ensure that the money you do have is working for you. Few people think of a business as having a savings account, but the interest you earn is as valuable as working a few extra hours! Talk to your accountant for other ideas.

Obtain a Line of Credit for Your Business

As quickly as you can, talk to your banker about a line of credit. A good banker will understand the need and its connection to cash flow. During your start-up phase, you could use your home as collateral if your banker doesn't find equity in your company's reputation, accounts receivable, or contracts alone. A line of credit is invaluable during a tight spot. Generally a phone call to your bank will deposit the amount you request into your account the same day. You can pay back the loan on your terms, sometimes paying only the interest each month.

Use a Business Credit Card Wisely

A business credit card can delay a payment for up to forty-five days. For example, let's say your credit card statement runs from the first of the month to the end of the month. You purchase office supplies during the first week. The credit card company doesn't send your bill until the thirtieth of the month, and you have two weeks before it is due, on the fifteenth of the month. You have delayed payment for forty-five days from the date you purchased the supplies. This period can be longer if your credit card company gives you longer to pay or shorter if you make your purchase later in the month. No matter what the dates, a credit card can help cash flow. One word of caution: The best way to use a credit card is to pay the balance every month to avoid the huge interest rates of 14 percent, 18 percent, or even 21 percent. Don't run a credit bill up so high that you are stuck paying these high interest rates.

Compare Leasing and Purchase Rates Carefully

I have always been a "buy it with cash" kind of person to avoid the interest rates. In fact I was in business for ten years before I even considered leasing equipment. One year we needed a new copier and we were short of cash. I studied the leasing agreement. It compared favorably to a cash purchase when I considered the maintenance agreement and the outright purchase option at the end of the leasing period. Since that experience, I always make the comparisons.

Play Up Your Small-Business Status

If you are a small business, you can type "Small business. Please expedite payment." at the bottom of your invoices. We've never used this technique, but have been told that it works with empathetic accounts payable departments.

Act on Late Payments Immediately

Even when you stay on top of invoices and send them out in a timely way, late payments will create a cash-flow issue. First, determine why the payment is late. It can be any of the following reasons:

- The client did not receive the invoice.
- One or more of the organization's processes caused a delay.
- The client may be deliberately paying late to manage cash flow or for other reasons.

How do you deal with late payments? First, call the organization's accounts payable department to learn whether the invoice was received. If the organization is notoriously late, you may wish to call one week after you send it to ensure that it is in their hands.

_____

Act on late payments immediately.

_____

Next, call the client for whom you completed the work and ask if your work was satisfactory. Assuming that the answer is yes, say that the reason you were asking is that the payment is past due and you were wondering if it was being held up for anything for which you were responsible. This will usually result in your client taking some action to help expedite your payment.

Last, submit a second bill that includes a new date, a statement that this is a "second bill," and a late-payment charge identified on the bill. Often consultants want to give the client another chance and not add the late-payment charge. You can if there was an unusual processing problem. You should if the bill never arrived. However, if the payment is more than a week late without good reason, submit a second invoice with the additional late fee added.

What amount should be charged for the late payment? Charge 1 to 2 percent per month. The very last line on our invoices reads, "A late payment charge of $1\frac{1}{2}$ percent will be assessed for all bills over 30 days." Some consultants use a ten- or fifteen-day payment schedule. If you choose something other than the conventional thirty days, it should be spelled out in the agreement or contract you have with the client.

Pay Bills When They Are Due, Not Before

Have you ever received a bill to renew a magazine when the subscription still had four months left? This is a common practice. Watch the due dates on bills for professional organizations, magazines, clubs, and others whose process is to bill you three or four months before the due date. You can file the bill you receive for later payment or even toss it! My professional organization bills me four times before they really expect payment.

Compare Actual Expenses to the Budget Monthly

Use a form similar to the one in Exhibit 6.1 to keep you informed about the status of your expenses: What's been paid, what's due this month, and which categories are ahead or behind budget? The amounts may be a real guessing game your first year, but it is a learning tool. The amounts for the second year will be more accurate if based on your first year's final totals.

TRACK EXPENSES

Where is all the money going? If you are not good at the details of bookkeeping, find someone else to do it for you. Although you are a consultant, you must also consider yourself a business owner. Tracking every expense is imperative. You may be lax about requesting and saving all those $2 parking receipts when you visit the library each week. Indeed, $2 does not seem like much. However, if you visit that library once or twice a week for resources, your parking receipts could easily add up to $150 worth of expenses. If your total state and federal tax bracket is 40 percent, you've just thrown away $60!

Now think about how many other things you might "forget" to record, such as tolls, business-related books or magazines, client gifts, mileage, seminar supplies you purchase on-site, office supplies you pick up on the weekend, light bulbs, cleaning supplies, or paper products you bring into the office from home.

What's the solution? Our consultants use envelopes for tracking expenses and for filing receipts. The 9"×12" envelopes identify the consultant, the client, the date, and a list of the expenses. We had a printer print several thousand for a very reasonable cost. They serve several purposes: They provide a place to put the receipts while we are collecting them; they provide a method for tracking expenses by client, even if we are in the same city for two separate clients; and they are neatly stored by project for easy retrieval at a later date if necessary.

In Chapter Four we listed items that might be in your monthly budget. These same budget line items are your expenses. You will want to track them for two reasons.

First, you will want to study them. Your expense record will provide the most information about your financial situation. It will tell you where you might cut

⊞ Exhibit 6.1. Monthly Expense/Worksheet Record.

Account	Budget	Jan	Feb	Mar	April	May	June	July	Aug	Sept	Oct	Nov	Dec	Total
Accounting, banking, legal fees														
Advertising and marketing														
Automobile expenses														
Books and resources														
Clerical support														
Copying and printing														
Donations														
Dues and subscriptions														
Entertainment														
Equipment leases														
Insurance														
Interest and loans														
Licenses														
Meals														
Office supplies														
Pension plan														
Postage														
Professional development														
Professional fees														
Rent														
Repairs and maintenance														
Resources														
Salaries														
Seminar expenses														
Taxes														
Telephone														
Travel														
Utilities														
Total														

back if you need to save, what you can expect in upcoming cash flow, and what you could prepay if you show too large a profit at the end of the year. (Perhaps the last item is surprising after the discussion about tight cash flow. You should assume that you will be so successful that you will face that problem in a year or two!)

The second reason you will want to track your expenses is to ensure that you can easily compile your records prior to filing your taxes. You will want to claim as many legitimate deductions as possible because it reduces your tax bill. Poor record keeping takes cash out of your pocket.

The monthly expense record in Exhibit 6.1 will be valuable for tracking your monthly expenses. The following categories identify where your money will go.

Accounting, Legal, and Banking Fees. Find an accountant as one of your first tasks. Good accountants will save you five times what they cost. There is no way (unless you are an accounting consultant) that you can keep up with all the tax law changes. For example, this year a new "Simplified SEP IRA" was offered. My accountant let me know about it and helped me decide whether I should maintain the pension plan I had for my employees or switch to the new one. You will have few legal fees beyond your initial incorporation, but you will likely have some minor monthly banking charges.

Advertising and Marketing. Initially, you will have the expense of printing a brochure or introductory piece to let people know who you are and what your capabilities are. I started out with a simple one-page introduction printed on good quality stationery. I never have completed a "mailing" of our corporate brochure, but it is useful as an introduction piece or as something to leave when I visit a potential client. Expenses here may include a special announcement mailing, books or articles you purchase to send to clients or potential clients, or marketing firm expenses you may incur.

Automobile. Establish a good tracking system for your automobile expenses. If you use the same vehicle for personal and business use, you will most likely track mileage only. The best way to handle this is to keep a clipboard with a form that allows you to track date, destination, purpose, beginning and ending odometer readings, and total mileage. Remember, you cannot deduct mileage going to and from your office. If you visit a client first, you cannot count that first leg of your trip either. Your accountant will assist you with the nuances of mileage.

Copying and Printing. If you do not purchase or lease your own copy machine, build a good relationship with the employees of your local copy center. There will be days when you will need a rush job!

Donations. Your business may make monetary or equipment donations to local charities. We donated a lettering machine to our local Head Start and old computers and software to the Salvation Army. Both were in good condition, but we had outgrown their use.

Dues and Subscriptions. Dues to professional organizations and subscriptions to professional journals are tax deductible.

Entertainment. Although you can only deduct 50 percent of the expense incurred when you take a client to dinner, you must still track it and maintain receipts. Track the full amount. Your accountant will take care of the reduction.

Equipment and Furniture Purchases. You may think this is only a one-time purchase, but you may upgrade computers or need a new desk sooner than you think. Depending on the amount you purchase or on your financial situation at the end of the year, your accountant may suggest that you depreciate the expense over several years to capture the greatest tax advantage.

Equipment and Furniture Leases. Be sure to check the advantages of leasing against purchasing. Sometimes it's just a matter of preference, but there also may be savings with one or the other.

Insurance. This is a broad category and may include fleet insurance if you own a company vehicle, fire and theft if you rent or own an office, group health if you have employees, business liability insurance, disability insurance, and a number of others. Again, your accountant is the best source for determining which would be better as business expenses and which would be better as personal expenses. For example, we have group health insurance for employees, but the law does not allow me to include my insurance as a business expense. Although my employees do not need to claim the premiums as income, as the owner, I do. I prefer to declare them as a personal expense to keep recording cleaner.

Interest and Loans. You may have taken out a loan to start your business. The interest is tax deductible. Although the principle is not deductible, it will still appear as an expense affecting your cash flow. By the way, even if you loaned yourself the money to start your business, you should track it.

Licenses. Check into state or city licenses that are required to do business in your city.

Meals. Local meals are tax deductible when they are business-related. In addition, keep all receipts for food when you travel. Again, as with the entertainment category, only 50 percent of the actual cost is tax deductible. Your accountant will assist you with this process at tax time.

Office Supplies. This category includes things such as paper supplies, ink cartridges for your printer, rubber bands, pens, paper towels, glass cleaner (to clean your copier's glass), floor mats, light bulbs, and anything else that it takes to keep an office operating.

Pension Plan. Excellent plans exist for small businesses. Check into them soon, even if you don't think you can afford it.

Postage. This is of course the cost of sending proposals, marketing materials, and other correspondence using the postal service or private carriers.

Professional Development. Stay current with the changes in your field. This category includes the costs for conferences, training, or local professional meetings you may attend.

Professional Fees. This category is for subcontractors you may hire to assist you with larger projects.

Rent. Track your office rent expense in this category.

Repairs and Maintenance. Often these expenses are included in an office lease. However, you may need to hire your own cleaning firm. In addition, if you own your computers, copier, and fax machines their repairs will be tracked in this category.

Resources. Keep up on the latest books in your field. A good library is a real time saver when it comes to developing new materials or writing proposals.

Salaries. Pay yourself first. You've heard that advice before. This category also includes anyone else you have hired such as your secretary, receptionist, assistant, or professionals who are on your payroll.

Seminar Expense. You may need to purchase a videotape to use during a training session. You may have some materials that you use in your sessions. For example, I use crayons, play dough, clay, jump ropes, and other toys in my creativity sessions.

Taxes. This category may include local business taxes, personal property taxes, unemployment taxes, self-employment taxes, FICA, and other payroll taxes.

Telephone. Telephone calls, fax transmissions, and your e-mail expenses are listed here.

Travel. Travel expenses include taxi fares, air fares, hotel rooms, shuttle buses, parking, tips, and other costs incurred as a result of getting to and staying at a site to conduct business. The expense report in Exhibit 6.2 will help you to track travel and other out-of-pocket expenses you incur throughout the month.

Utilities. Electricity, water, heat, or air conditioning may be included in your office rent. If you are working out of your home, your accountant will assist you to determine what percentage of the total you can consider a business expense.

Breaking expenses into categories like this creates a system that makes it easy for you to track expenses, manage cash flow, and predict revenue needed for next month as well as next year.

SET ASIDE PETTY CASH

If you find yourself digging into your own pocket to pay for postage or other small purchases during the month, you may wish to create a petty cash fund. Having cash on hand eliminates the need for you to record every little expense for reimbursement. To establish the fund, write a check out to petty cash. Keep the money in a safe place, but separate from your personal money. The form in Exhibit 6.3 provides an easy way to track these expenditures.

Exhibit 6.2. Time Sheet and Expense Report.

Name: _____ Work Period: _____

Date	Activity	Mileage		Other Travel Expenses*			Employee Tax Record
		Specify	Miles	@.35	Travel	Lodging	Meals	Gross =
								– State Tax
								– Federal Tax
								– SS Tax
								+ Expenses
								– Deductions
								Net =

Miscellaneous*

Specify	Amount

Totals

Signature: _____   Date: _____   *Attach Receipts in Expense Envelope   Expense Total: _____

💾 Exhibit 6.3. Petty Cash Record.

				From: _____	To: _____
Date	Where Bought	Item(s) Purchased	Expense Category	Initial	Amount
				Total	

CHARGE YOUR CLIENT

In general, consultants are not very confident about what we charge our clients. Perhaps this is due to the many jokes and cartoons referencing consultants and their fees. I remember how difficult it was to state my fee when I first raised it to $1,000. "I charge one th-th-th-thousand dollars a day," I would stutter. Certainly the exercise in Chapter Three showing how easily a $1,500 daily charge can accumulate should allow you to feel more confident. Although it is important that *we* know that our prices are fair and value-filled, it is even more important that *our clients* be satisfied that they receive value for their investment.

If consultants have difficulty in stating our fees, we have even more difficulty in ensuring that our clients know what we did for them. Granted, much of our work can be elusive, intangible, and invisible, but that does not mean that it is not valuable. Keep your work in front of your clients—not bragging, but informing. Try these suggestions:

- Itemize your invoice to include specific accomplishments.

- Itemize things you did without charge and specify the amount as $0.00. We often list books we have provided at no extra charge or an unscheduled meeting.

- Submit your invoice in person, discussing what it covers.

- When on-site, save the end of your day to update your client about recent activities and their results.

- Submit a brief ongoing status report if visits are not practical.

- When your client requests something special, follow up personally with the results.

- Keep the client informed of what is happening behind the scenes. What should the client expect to see or hear?

- Make a phone call during extended time periods to stay in the loop and to show that you care.

- Send books or articles. We all read something and think that it is perfect reading for a particular client. Make it possible by sending it!

Each of these ideas ensures that you keep your client informed of the value you are adding to the organization.

Invoices

As mentioned previously in this chapter, issuing invoices should be one of your top priorities. They should be submitted as soon as the project has ended. If the project's duration is greater than thirty days, bill monthly or every two weeks for deliverables you have completed, plus the expenses incurred. This is best for you and for your client. You prevent cash-flow problems; your client will find it easier to pay several small invoices each month than one large one after four months. The invoicing summary in Exhibit 6.4 provides an easy method to track the date you invoiced the client, what services you invoiced for, and the date the client's payment was received.

Keep your client informed of the value
you are adding to the organization.

Your invoice should provide all the information necessary for a client to quickly approve payment. Include these items:

- Your corporate name, address, and telephone number (During start-up use your stationery rather than have actual invoices printed).
- A numbering system for tracking invoices.
- The billing date.
- The address and the name of the person to whom the invoice is sent.
- An itemized list of the tasks completed, dates, and hours if appropriate.
- The name of the person completing the tasks.
- A list of the expenses incurred.
- Total of the entire invoice.
- Terms of the invoice, such as due date and consequences of late payments.
- Your Federal ID number or your Social Security number.
- The name of the person to whom questions may be addressed (optional).

In addition to the invoice, attach copies of receipts incurred as expenses, for example, a hotel bill, meal receipt, or copy-center invoice. Although your client may not require these receipts, I believe it builds trust and is a good practice. Exhibit 6.5 is a simple, yet complete invoice format.

◫ Exhibit 6.4. Invoice Summary.

Work Date	Organization	Trainer	Invoice Number	Billed	Paid	Facilitator Fee	Materials Fee	Expenses	Total Fee
Total									

⊞ Exhibit 6.5. Invoice.

INVOICE

100-000111-2000

TO: Ms. Joan Smith
                Head Start Association
                333 Ridge Road
                Anywhere, NY 10000

Invoice Date: January 24, 2001

For: Presented "Total Quality Management Applied: Learning
                from Our Experience" for the Head Start Association on
                November 15, 2000.
                Elizabeth Drake, Facilitator
                        Facilitator Fee . . . . $ 2,000.00

EXPENSES: Mileage Round Trip to Airport:
                        80 miles @$.35 per mile . . . . $ 28.00
                Airfare . . . . $ 381.00
                Airport parking . . . . $ 20.00
                Lodging . . . . $ 70.00
                Books . . . . $ 0.00
                        Expense Total . . . . $ 499.00

Amount Due: . . . . $ 2,499.00

Terms: Due upon receipt

Payable to: ebb associates
                Box 657
                Portage, WI 53901

                Federal ID# 33-5333788

2 percent late fee charged per month for accounts due over 15 days

The Clients' Expenses

For what expenses can you expect the client to be responsible? In almost all cases the client will reimburse all travel expenses incurred when you are away from home: Air fare, taxis, mileage to and from the airport, parking, reasonable lodging, meals, and tips. If you have agreed to it, a client may also cover materials costs, audiovisual equipment and materials (for example, video rental), seminar supplies, room rental, or refreshments. Depending on the industry you serve and your pricing structure, your client may also reimburse you for telephone or fax expenses, overnight mail, computer time, or computer program development. We consider telephone calls and faxes a cost of doing business and include them as a part of our overhead.

Do not expect a client to cover laundry, dry cleaning, liquor, upgraded hotel rooms, entertainment, or unrelated phone calls when you travel. Local travel and meals are not reimbursable. Postage is not generally reimbursed, unless you have a large mailing to send as a part of the contract.

In any event, all reimbursables should be clearly spelled out at the beginning of any contract.

PROJECT REVENUES

As important as tracking expenses is projecting revenue. We project revenues by the month. This works for us because we have been able to adjust our accounting processes so that we pay bills only once each month. You may wish to track revenue weekly, especially if cash flow is a concern. The revenue projection form in Exhibit 6.6 can be transferred to a spreadsheet so that you can keep a running total by month as well as by organization.

DEAL WITH BAD DEBTS

Bad debts occur when your clients do not pay you for the services provided. They occur infrequently in the consulting business, although when they do they can be devastating to a small business. Although we have never experienced a bad debt, we have heard that professional firms can experience bad debt rates from 5 to 30 percent.

If this should occur, you may use a collection agency to assist you. In some cases, you may choose to take the matter to your local small claims court. They are generally well informed and very helpful.

▣ Exhibit 6.6. Revenue Projections.

Organization and Project	Jan	Feb	Mar	April	May	June	July	Aug	Sept	Oct	Nov	Dec	Total
Total Revenue													

KEEP AN EYE ON YOUR NUMBERS

Although you are a consultant, you should never forget that you are running a business. Businesses exist to make a profit. The numbers will spell profit or loss for your business. You must establish processes for gathering the numbers and then keep an eye on them. As a good business owner you will want to know where you stand financially at any given time. That means that you must read the numbers, compare them, and play with them. Read them and know what they mean. Increases? Decreases? Compare them to the last project, last month, last year. Are they better? Worse? And finally, play with them. What if you invested in a new computer system? Prepaid bills before the end of the year?

Never forget that you are running a business.

What specifically can you look for when you are studying your numbers?

Expenses

Certainly you should compare your actual expenditures with your budget. Are you over? Under? Both are worthy of investigation. If the actual is over the budget, look at the detailed report. What pushed you over the limit? Is it likely to occur again? Should you adjust your budget to account for the difference? What about being under budget? That's good so don't worry. Right? Wrong! If you have budgeted for something and the money wasn't spent, you need to examine this as well. Perhaps a marketing mailing you budgeted for was not done. This may affect income several months down the road.

Businesses exist to make a profit.

It could be worse. Once I discovered an extra $400 in the budget. First I felt smug; then I became curious. When I finally discovered what had caused the difference, I panicked. The fire insurance on our new office building had not been paid! Remember, being under budget can be as bad as being over budget.

Value

Compare some of your expenses to the time invested to determine if the value is warranted. For example, you have hired two associates to help you deliver services and now find yourself doing the payroll every other week. Your receptionist is stretched and you cannot justify hiring a bookkeeper. So you do the payroll. Check into the payroll services that abound. They do it all: Figure salaries, compute the taxes, write the checks, deposit the taxes, and provide monthly as well as year-end reports and W-2s. And they do it for a reasonable fee. Consider the time you are investing in payroll or any other administrative task. Is it the best use of your time? Is this where you should invest your value?

Growth

You will certainly be comparing income to expenses, but you should also watch the overall growth trend. Is the number of projects increasing? Is your gross income growing proportionately? Are expenses growing at the same, greater, or lesser rate? You might think that growth is always desired. That isn't so. It is not desired if you have over-scheduled yourself. It is not desired if you have decided not to hire employees. It is not desired if the projects are less profitable. And it certainly is not desired if you are working harder and enjoying it less.

Exhibit 6.7 is a form for you to track time and materials used on individual projects. Exhibit 6.8 provides a method for recording and comparing the profitability of various projects. This can assist you to determine which projects are the most profitable and can assist you with bidding on new projects.

Certainly, growth can be exactly what you desire and what you have planned for. Given that, there is still one more thing to watch for. Fast growth can lead to cash-flow issues. You may need to invest in new projects up front that are not in your budget. Check the cash-flow suggestions earlier in this chapter and keep an eye on the numbers.

CONSIDER CAPITAL INVESTMENTS

You are running a business. That means that you have capital investments, and with that goes responsibility. If you own equipment, put each item on a preventive maintenance schedule. Clean phones, computers, copiers, printers, and other

🖫 Exhibit 6.7. Project Time and Expense Record.

Date	Team Member	Task Performed or Materials Used	Hours or Expense	Salary or Cost

◧ Exhibit 6.8. Program Development Costs versus Revenue.

Program Title	Company	Work Date	Production Hours	Production Cost	$ Charged

equipment regularly. You will benefit in the long run. Equipment will last longer and it will not be "down" just when you need it to complete the last-minute details of a program you will conduct the next day!

Your library is a capital investment that can easily walk out the door without your vigilance. We have a complete library that can easily compete with any area library in the training, business, consulting, management, quality, and communication categories. Many of our local clients and other consultants, as well as employees, borrow volumes from it. Although we want to share the resources, a library sign-out sheet allows us to do so without worrying about unreturned books. Exhibit 6.9 is a copy of that form.

💾 **Exhibit 6.9. Library Sign-Out Sheet.**

Book	Borrowed By	Date	Will Return By	Returned

This chapter should have driven home the importance of tracking and monitoring your income and expenses. You could be the best consultant in the world, but if you do not make money, you will not remain in business, and the world will never know about your consulting expertise!

Building a Client Relationship

*"Hold yourself responsible for a higher standard than
anybody expects of you. Never excuse yourself."*

Henry Ward Beecher

You started your business to serve clients. Serve them well! This can only happen if you are continually aware of building the relationship you have with each of your clients.

Your initial contact with a new client is more important than you can imagine. Your comfort with one another and your ability to communicate clearly and candidly are critical to start on the right foot.

The success of your interactions and the results of your project will establish and build your relationship and help you to maintain a client for a long time. There is an interesting phenomenon that the longer you have clients, the longer they will continue to be clients. Now mind you, this is not about building a client's reliance on you. It is about a client who thinks of you whenever a new project comes up. With the frequent changes that businesses go through today, that can be often.

———————

You started your business to serve clients.

———————

In these relationships you become too valuable to lose. Your knowledge of the organization, your rapport with key managers, and your experience with the political and operational factors of the organization cannot be replaced—at any cost. Why would you want to encourage repeat business?

1. Repeat business means you will not need to expend time marketing your services. The client knows you—knows your capabilities and how you might help. Also, because you know the client, there will be less lag time from the time the client hires you to the time you begin the project.

2. He or she will call you regularly to assist in many different situations. Each will build on past projects, and you will continue to increase in value. We are frequently referred from department to department or from division to division.

3. You will have a leg up against your competition. You have already built a relationship with the client. The trust you have built will count heavily on your side when the need arises.

4. You will not lose clients during difficult economic times. In fact, your expertise may be readily called on to help them through.

5. You will develop a valuable marketing vehicle. A client's referral is the most potent marketing tool you can have. If your project is successful and you have built solid relationships, your clients will refer you to others. Our clients market us to other organizations. This happens because we pay attention both to doing the job with quality results and to building the relationship. I am firmly convinced that without the effort we put into building the relationship this would not occur.

So how can you get to a point at which your clients market you? First, you must find the project; your first meeting will most likely determine that. Next, you must build the relationship. Every interaction, every product, and every result will make a difference. Finally, you must maintain the relationship. The project ends, not the relationship. Your follow-up will maintain the relationship.

The project ends,
not the relationship.

THE FIRST MEETING

Your initial meeting is critical. It sets a tone for the rest of the relationship, which is why it is important to be yourself in this meeting. Many consultants come prepared for their initial introduction with a "dog and pony show"—a slick PowerPoint® presentation, materials in a bound folder, and a precisely worded presentation. If that's your style and it works for you, continue doing it. We try to create a conversation with the client; that's our style. It's natural and it sets the tone for the rest of the relationship. How do we fare? Recently we were pitted against three of the top ten consulting firms in the United States. We were awarded the job. Be yourself. If you land the project, it will be difficult to continue the charade you used to get it.

The skills you need for this first meeting read like an Interpersonal Skills 101 class:

- Read the client to determine whether to make small talk first or to get right down to business. Attending to the client's communication style will lay a foundation for the rest of the discussion.
- Listen for understanding, especially to determine the critical points. Sometimes clients will not be clear about what they want. Read between the lines and interpret meaning or structure the content to make sense of the situation. Remember that every statement has at least two messages: The content and the intent.
- Ask pertinent and thought-provoking questions. Before you attend the meeting, develop three to ten questions based on what you know about the situation. Three well-thought-out questions will usually start a discussion. You will probably not have time to ask ten questions, and if you have more than ten, it will be difficult to prioritize while you're trying to focus.
- Put others at ease by remembering and using their names, by showing interest in their needs, and by balancing the discussion appropriately in a group. Ask for a list of attendees and their positions for your first meeting. Study the names before the meeting. After you are introduced, subtly make a seating chart as a reference. Then use people's names throughout the meeting.
- Exude self-confidence without arrogance. You will display your self-confidence with your body language as much as anything, so use good eye contact, a pleasant demeanor, and confident posture. The client will want to know about your past experience. Providing examples or relating similar situations should be

a natural part of the discussion. Take care to avoid bragging, giving too much detail, or sounding as if you have rehearsed a rote speech.

- Project a professional image. First impressions count. A firm handshake, appropriate attire, and genuine interest in the client and the organization you are visiting will help you make a great first impression.

Your personality, not your expertise, will land most contracts. That may disappoint you, but it is the truth. Sure, you must have the basic skills in place, but that's a given. Your wit, charm, sincerity, professionalism, or interpersonal skills will be the deciding factor at this stage.

A quick measure of how you're doing can be determined by how much you are talking. If the clients are doing the majority of the talking, it's a sign that they feel comfortable with you and that you are asking appropriate questions. If you are doing more talking, more selling than listening, your chances of successfully landing this contract are decreasing.

Your personality,
not your expertise,
will land most contracts.

FOUR PHASES OF BUILDING A CLIENT-CONSULTANT PARTNERSHIP

The relationship you begin to establish during the first meeting lays the groundwork for a solid client-consultant partnership—in which both the client and the consultant are equal, contributing counterparts in an effort to accomplish a mutual goal.

Building a partnership with your client may be similar to building a friendship or a team. Let's explore building a client-consultant partnership in four phases: (1) finding the right match, (2) getting to know one another, (3) being productive, and (4) creating independence.

Phase I focuses on finding the right match and deciding whether you and the client can work together. When you are introduced to someone, you make decisions about whether you want to pursue a relationship. Even though you and your client may already be discussing the project, a final decision about how to move forward has not been made. I have been in this phase for as little as ten minutes and as long as a couple of months.

Phase II focuses on getting to know one another. At this point a commitment exists to move the project to the next level. The relationship is moving forward as well. Both parties are learning everything they can about one another and how to work together effectively.

Phase III occurs when you and your client are productive. The project is in full swing. If you and your client have worked on the relationship, your partnership is in full swing as well.

Phase IV focuses on helping the client to become independent. The project is coming to a close. By focusing on the client's independence, you ensure that his or her organization continues to be successful. Equally as important, you ensure that your relationship continues to be healthy.

Phase I: Finding the Right Match

During this phase, you will focus on two areas: Obtaining information and setting expectations. Both lead to a final decision about whether to move forward with the project.

Getting Information. Prior to meeting someone of interest, you may ask questions and try to gather information about them. Prior to meeting a client, you may choose to obtain the best public information available about the organization and the industry. How? Ask people. Go to the library. Check the industry journals. Find the client company's most recent annual report.

If you are meeting someone from an industry that is new to you, become familiar with the general industry jargon. Reading several industry journals will help.

This is also the time to define the scope of the effort. Your client may not be able to answer all questions at this time, but it is important that you clarify the scope as much as possible. You may find that the project is larger than you want to take on.

We've found it valuable to discuss past projects for which the client used consultants. Answers to simple questions such as, "What went well?" and "What would you do differently?" provide information about how the client likes to work.

Your client will be obtaining information from you, too. Be prepared to provide references, and encourage the client to call them. Speaking with your former clients gives a potential client confidence in your abilities. Last, discuss your consulting fee and how you invoice.

Setting Expectations. Establishing expectations between you and your client lays a solid foundation for the relationship. The process is often referred to as "contracting."

Contracting is the process by which you and your client identify, clarify, and agree on both of your needs, wants, and expectations. Contracting is critical in the first phase, because it is here that you and your client will begin to build your partnership, begin to clarify the project, and begin to understand and appreciate one another's principles, styles, and values.

Peter Block, in his best-selling classic, *Flawless Consulting,* explains contracting as the process to reach "an explicit agreement of what the consultant and client expect from each other and how they are going to work together." Your contracting discussion should explore and come to agreement on things such as the following:

- Your role, the client's role, and how they are related.
- The project's time frame.
- The expected outcome of the project.
- The support, resources, and information you will need from the client.
- How this project fits into the larger organizational picture and the organization's vision.

As a result of this discussion, you should have a better idea of the client's ability to support the effort; some of the values that you share and where you differ; the client's vision for the project; the organization's support for the project; and your desire to complete the project.

In addition, you should have determined who your primary client is. The primary client is most often the individual who hired you for the project, but on a few rare occasions another department, human resources for example, may actually bring you in and provide the budget for work you conduct in another department.

You will also have secondary clients and stakeholders. They are the individuals who are affected by your work, but are not directing it.

Exhibit 7.1 identifies a list of questions you can ask yourself. Use it in two ways: It was designed for you to evaluate your behavior after the contracting meeting and to use it before the meeting as a reminder of all the things you must remember during the meeting.

💾 Exhibit 7.1. Contracting Checklist.

Evaluate the contracting meeting with your client.

Did I:

		Yes	No
1.	Do my homework before the meeting?	❏	❏
2.	Determine the primary client?	❏	❏
3.	Determine the secondary clients and stakeholders?	❏	❏
4.	Define the scope of the effort?	❏	❏
5.	Elicit the clients' specific needs and expectations?	❏	❏
6.	Identify shared values and differences?	❏	❏
7.	Evaluate the client's expertise and ability to support the effort?	❏	❏
8.	Discuss my rates and consulting approach?	❏	❏
9.	Clearly state my needs and expectations?	❏	❏
10.	Obtain a sense of client commitment to the effort?	❏	❏
11.	Provide references?	❏	❏

Asking Questions. Questions represent the means by which the client and consultant determine if they have found the right match. Either you or the client may find the following questions helpful.

- What are your mission, vision, and guiding principles?
- What values are most important to your organization?
- What resources are available (time, people, space)?
- What observation opportunities exist (consultant in action, meetings, work processes)?
- How will we conduct a front-end analysis and what type?
- What options are available to work through a relationship problem?
- What logistics do we need to clarify (shared copyright, scheduling, reporting)?

Additional questions you might ask to learn more about the organization include these:

- How do you feel about my being brought into the organization?
- What's it like to work here?
- How will this organization be different as a result of this intervention?

Phase II: Getting To Know One Another

When you build relationships with individuals, you spend time getting to know them. You can do the same thing with your clients. This phase is typically considered the data-collection step in consulting. It is natural that, as you build the relationship, you learn everything you can about the client. You learned things about the client in Phase I, but now you are on-site, asking questions, touring plants, observing meetings, interviewing employees, or eating in the corporate dining room.

As with a personal relationship, the more you know about the organization, the better you will understand its people, its problems, and its culture. Every time you interview key employees of the organization, you influence the relationship. You will be gaining information about the organization's attitudes, skills, and climate.

During this phase you have the opportunity to invest in the relationship by modeling appropriate skills. Every interaction is an opportunity to model good communication, teamwork, and high-quality work. The relationship benefits in two ways: You gain respect from the client and the client has an opportunity to observe professional skills.

Initial planning takes place during Phase II. You will provide an analysis of the situation, recommendations, and a plan for proceeding. You will reach consensus around the plan as well as on how to keep the client informed. Provide ample opportunity for milestones, progress reports, and other communication that will keep the client informed of progress. Maintaining an open line of communication will continue to build the relationship. If you spend the time getting to know the people and the organization, you will begin to build a trusting relationship.

Phase III: Being Productive

Several books have been written about how to manage an external consultant. Chances are good that your client has not read any of these books and will be expecting you to manage the project and the relationship. During this implementation stage, you have the opportunity to continue to build the relationship through what you deliver and how you deliver your services.

What You Deliver. All clients I have worked with believe that they are special and that their business is unique. Perhaps that's human nature. Although you will find plenty of similarities from client to client, you must still study the situation with an open mind. Look for the differences. That allows you to create customized solutions for the client more easily.

You will probably need to conduct one-on-one coaching sessions. Be honest and helpful. Building the relationship does not mean that you will agree with everything the individual does or says. In fact, once individuals reach a certain level, they rarely receive candid feedback from anyone within the organization. How many employees give feedback to the president?

Become an active member of the client's team. You can do more as a part of the team than by maintaining your separateness. Become involved. Be aware of the "magic wand" syndrome. Some clients may believe that you have arrived to "fix things." Permanent fixes only occur if you and the client work together in a partnership.

Things will go wrong. You will uncover things you wish you had not. The unexpected will occur. In every instance, be honest, candid, and timely about issues, problems, and concerns. Don't be afraid to say, "It's not working." Keep the right person informed. Your honesty and candor will be respected by everyone.

While you're in the thick of implementation, it may be difficult to focus on the day when you will no longer be involved in the project. However, this is the ideal time to plan for the skills your client will need to ensure continued success. Your client will brag about you if you make this happen. That means you must attend to it now through coaching, teaching, and mentoring. Continually create ways that lead to the client's independence.

Communicate, communicate, communicate! Keep everyone informed. You will not be able to communicate too much. Guaranteed! Find many ways to keep employees informed, such as memos, e-mail, posters, telephone trees, town meetings, presentations, Q & A sessions, and paycheck stuffers. Help your client develop a communication plan.

How You Deliver Services. As in any business, how you deliver your services is as important as the service you provide. Build your relationship with your client by providing superb service. As with any business, the eight commonly accepted elements of service that follow apply to your consulting practice.

1. *Time.* How much time are you spending on the project? Too little and your clients will wonder what they are paying for; too much and your clients will wonder if you have moved in! In addition, plan time to build the client relationship. It's a key element in delivering high-quality service.

2. *Timeliness.* Do you do what you say you are going to do when you say you will? Do you return your phone calls promptly?

3. *Completeness.* Do you do everything you say you will? Do you do everything you should do? Always?

4. *Courtesy.* Do you treat everyone in your client's firm respectfully, politely, and cheerfully? Do you greet the receptionist with the same positive attention with which you greet the CEO?

5. *Consistency.* Do you provide the same high quality services to all clients and to every department and to everyone within each organization?

6. *Convenience.* Are you easy to reach? Are you able to turn on a dime to meet special needs that may come up?

7. *Accuracy.* Is your service provided right the first time? Do you aim for "flawless consulting?" Do the results demonstrate the accuracy that was agreed on initially?

8. *Responsiveness.* How quickly do you respond if something goes awry? Do you accept the responsibility for problems?

Phase IV: Creating Independence

As the excitement of the project winds down and you complete your final tasks with the client, you may not feel as enthusiastic about the project as you did when you started. This is natural, something like the post-holiday letdown that sometimes occurs. Some consultants avoid this unpleasant feeling by focusing on their next clients. They just drift away. This is unfair to your client. Finish the project completely. Maintain your standards of quality.

You still have work to do. Although you should have been building your client's independence throughout the project, this is the time to confirm that the client has the tools and skills to continue without you. You may want to ensure that trainers are certified to teach ongoing classes, that supervisors are comfortable using the new computer program, that the project manager knows where to obtain additional information and support, or that the internal coaches know how to use the resources you designed for them.

You will want to ensure that the client knows to contact you with questions or concerns after the project has ended. We tell our clients that they can't get rid of us! What we mean by that is that our initial consulting fee grants them the privilege to call us at any time with questions, when they need ideas, if they need advice, or if they just need to vent.

There is a fine line between making the client dependent on you and providing help when it is really needed. After you have worked with a client and know him or her well, it's easy to provide additional ideas and support.

During this phase you will want to discuss continued communication. Identify who will be the best point of contact for future communication or follow-up. Let your client know that you will continue to maintain contact by sending articles, books, or notes and with periodic phone calls. Find out what the client's needs are as well.

Celebrate the project's success with your client. Celebrations are a great way to establish closure to the project. You could take the client to lunch or give a small gift that represents the partnership you have developed.

When you return to your office, don't forget to send a follow-up note thanking your client for the business and the opportunity to provide service.

Exhibits 7.2 and 7.3 provide two Client-Consultant Partnership Checklists— one for you and one for your client. These can serve as reminders for what you can do during each phase to build the relationship or can serve as discussion starters for you and your client during the early part of your relationship.

🖫 Exhibit 7.2. Client-Consultant Partnership: Consultant Checklist.

Phase I: Finding the Right Match

❑ Obtain the best public information available about the organization and the industry
❑ Learn general industry jargon
❑ Define the scope of the effort
❑ Require that client specifically define expectations and who does what
❑ Evaluate client's ability to support the effort
❑ Identify shared values/differences
❑ Identify client's vision for the project
❑ Provide rates and anticipated invoicing plan
❑ Obtain feeling for organization's support
❑ Provide references
❑ Discuss previous consultant efforts and biases

Phase II: Getting To Know One Another

❑ Learn everything possible about the client
❑ Get inside the organization to understand its culture
❑ Interview key people
❑ Develop baseline information about attitudes, skills, climate
❑ Model skills at every opportunity
❑ Provide an initial plan
❑ Build consensus around the plan
❑ Plan for milestones, progress reports, communication

Phase III: Being Productive

❑ Study the situation with an open mind
❑ Create customized solutions
❑ Conduct one-on-one coaching sessions
❑ Become an active member of the client's team
❑ Determine client self-sufficiency needs for the future
❑ Be aware of the "magic wand" syndrome
❑ Be honest, candid, and timely with issues and concerns
❑ Continually create ways that lead to the client's independence
❑ Communicate, communicate, communicate!

Phase IV: Creating Independence

❑ Validate self-sufficiency
❑ Develop a system of continued communication
❑ Determine best point of contact for future communication or follow-up
❑ Continue to maintain contact with articles, books, notes, periodic contact
❑ Celebrate success with the client

🖫 Exhibit 7.3. Client-Consultant Partnership: Client Checklist.

Phase I: Finding the Right Match

- ❏ Meet with lead consultants
- ❏ Request a proposal to ensure that the consultant understands the situation
- ❏ Learn about the consultant's company
- ❏ Contact references and past clients
- ❏ Obtain information: how long in business, consultants' backgrounds, type of clients served, repeat business, general reputation
- ❏ Observe consultant in action, if possible
- ❏ Check consultant's experience in your industry
- ❏ Identify shared values/differences
- ❏ Determine capabilities versus needs
- ❏ Determine flexibility/availability of consultant
- ❏ Clarify specific expectations and who does what
- ❏ Identify desired time frame
- ❏ Discuss limitations (money, time)
- ❏ Discuss known/suspected roadblocks
- ❏ Think in terms of a long-term relationship: Is rapport evident? Is there a personal fit?

Phase II: Getting To Know One Another

- ❏ Choose one person as point of contact
- ❏ Include consultant on the team
- ❏ Ask the consultant to help identify the problem as well as the solution
- ❏ Provide telephone directory, rosters
- ❏ Add to in-house mailing list for newsletters, updates
- ❏ Add to distribution list for pertinent teams
- ❏ Provide feedback on employees' initial reactions to the project
- ❏ Discuss risk factors

Phase III: Being Productive

- ❏ Establish regular feedback sessions
- ❏ Develop tracking system for continuity
- ❏ Be honest and candid with information and concerns
- ❏ Communicate, communicate, communicate!

Phase IV: Creating Independence

- ❏ Validate self-sufficiency
- ❏ Ensure that a system of continued communication is in place
- ❏ Ensure that management is aware of next steps
- ❏ Continue to provide news, success stories
- ❏ Keep consultant on mailing list
- ❏ Request advice if issues arise
- ❏ Plan success celebration

HOW TO IMPROVE THE RELATIONSHIP CONTINUOUSLY

A sale is not something you close; it closes itself while you are busy serving your customer. Having a positive relationship with your client makes it easier to close your next sale, due to referrals. Do such a good job of completing the project and building the relationship that your client brags about you.

A sale is not something you close;
it closes itself while you are busy
serving your customer.

What can you do so that your client will brag about you? The following ideas will help you start. Then think of twenty more that are unique to you.

- Deliver more than you promise.
- Make opportunities to meet as many employees as possible.
- Request copies of the organization's newsletter and telephone directory.
- Learn something personal about your most frequent contacts.
- Keep everyone informed; publicize project status as appropriate.
- Keep both company and individual information confidential.
- Arrive early, stay late.
- Adapt your work style to that of the organization.
- Meet all deadlines.
- Find ways to build trust.
- If you cannot meet a deadline, inform your clients as soon as you know and tell them why.
- Invite the client to shadow you when appropriate.
- Make the client feel like the "only" client.
- Send articles and share books that would be helpful to individuals.
- Be tough on the problem, but supportive of the person.
- Openly offer information about yourself.

- Explore a non-business related topic you both enjoy discussing.
- Discover common acquaintances.
- Discover locations where you have both lived or visited.
- Discover common experiences you have had.
- Write thank-you notes and how-are-you-doing notes.
- Call frequently when not on-site.
- Be available when not on-site.
- Follow through on special requests from individuals.
- Provide doughnuts for special meetings or if they're not in the client's budget.
- Offer and provide resources.
- Assist with developing outlines for future needs that support the effort.
- Send surprises, such as puzzles, posters, cartoons, or special overhead transparencies.
- Be prepared to help your client deal with the stress of change.
- Support your client. Find positive aspects in situations that he or she may not see.
- Avoid internal politics.
- Discuss the organization's successes, but also discuss your objective thoughts about what could be done better.
- Discuss small problems before they become big problems.
- Be prepared to deal with unplanned delays—cheerfully.
- Openly discuss delays caused by the client that may prevent you from meeting deadlines; resolve them with the client.
- Plan and work as partners.
- Give the client credit for success.
- Attend the organization's social functions.
- Coach on an individual basis.
- Teach by example.
- Ask for feedback.
- Apologize.
- Smile.

Decisions

Building a solid client relationship may create situations that require you to make decisions. The first situation is difficult: It is possible to become too friendly with your client. This prevents you from maintaining your objectivity. When that happens, ethically you will need to sever the professional relationship. This is definitely a drawback to building a solid client-consultant relationship and has happened to me several times. I've always decided that the long-term friendship was worth more than the business I lost.

Another decision you may need to make is of a more positive nature. You may receive job offers. If you are good at what you do, it's going to happen. A client respects your professional approach, admires your results, and enjoys working with you. These are the ingredients that lead to a job offer. This is the kind of validation that consultants appreciate. Do you want a job, or do you want to continue as a consultant? The decision is yours.

Communication

Even if you are being paid to give advice, listening is the most critical communication skill, both for completing the project and for building the relationship. Learn and use good questioning techniques so that you are asking the right questions in the right way. Neither a wimp nor an interrogator be! Learn and use paraphrasing, summarizing, and clarifying techniques.

Remember the critical role that nonverbals play in the communication process. You may wish to pair up with someone periodically who can give you feedback about the nonverbal messages you may be sending.

IT'S THE PEOPLE

Perhaps the most important aspect to remember about building a strong client-consultant relationship is that it's all about people. You are not really building a relationship with the client organization. You are building a relationship with the individuals within the organization.

You may be working on a project *for* ABC, Inc., but you are working *with* individuals like Jack and Ilona. ABC, Inc., may pay your consulting fee, but president Francis and receptionist Lee will determine whether you earned it by adding value. You may receive a referral from ABC, Inc., but Jose will write it.

Build a relationship with everyone in the organization. They are all important to the company. Building a relationship with all employees is equally as important as building a relationship with the president. Kowtowing to the president will be observed by the employees—and by the president. Don't do it.

For me, building a relationship with my client is equally as important as completing the project and exceeding the results my client expects. It is part of my philosophy of doing business. If building relationships is not a part of your business philosophy, you may want to review the beginning of this chapter. Reconsider the business value of building relationships.

HOW TO MAINTAIN THE RELATIONSHIP AFTER THE PROJECT

It would be foolish of you to ignore a relationship you have spent months to build. Many of the ideas in this chapter can be used to maintain a relationship after the project ends. Continue to stay in touch with your clients. You will find ways to maintain the relationship. Let me share some of the ways I do this.

- I purchase article reprints that will be interesting to my clients and send them on a regular basis.

- I stay in touch. I continue to send notes and cards. Usually I've learned a great deal about a client's likes, dislikes, pet peeves, hobbies, and interests. I may find items or reading materials about any of these. I find reasons to call them.

- If I find that I will be near a previous client's location, I will call the client and plan to have breakfast, lunch, dinner, or just a visit. I drop in and visit their business locations when I can.

- I encourage my clients to call at any time. I enjoy helping them find resources or materials. I enjoy helping them track down a bit of information or someone who could help them. They call to ask if I know of available jobs or people to fill job openings that they have. They call for recommendations about conferences or books. It is a sign of a solid partnership to have requests coming my way regularly.

- I sell my clients to others regularly. I find new customers for them. I recommend them to serve on boards. I sell their products. For example, Land O'Lakes is one of my clients. If a restaurant uses Land O'Lakes butter, I never hesitate to compliment them on using the best butter in the world.

- I also call clients if I need help. I call them if I know of available jobs. I may call them to serve as a resource for someone else or to ask if I can use their names as references. Always ask permission before you use a client as a reference for another project. Even this continues to maintain the relationship.

Maintaining the relationship can be whatever you decide it should be. We have lots of repeat work. I believe that is primarily due to providing high-quality, results-oriented consulting. However, I believe that a solid relationship makes it easier to remember us when new projects evolve.

We have other clients whom we simply enjoy staying in touch with. There is little chance that additional work will ensue. That isn't our primary reason for maintaining the relationship. We do it because we like to.

MORE VALUE FOR THE CLIENT

A successful client-consultant relationship provides more value for the client than the client expected. Think about how delighted you are when you receive more than what you expected: Fresh flowers in your hotel room, a complimentary mug with your breakfast buffet, a free chocolate sample with your bakery purchase, or a free car wash with your oil change. A relationship focus makes it easy to remember to add extras to the project that have value to the client but cost you little.

Building the client-consultant relationship is a process that takes time and energy. Building the relationship is equally as important as your expertise. Do it because you care. Caring—truly caring—is a powerful business advantage.

Growing Pains

"A goal is a dream with its feet on the ground."

Anonymous

All business owners reach a point at which they begin asking themselves questions about growth. Let's explore a few of the many opportunities for growth.

Perhaps the first question is "What does growth mean?" We can probably assume that it at least means more income. Does growth also mean more people in your organization? In what capacity? Do you want someone who replicates your skills? Compliments them? Do you want a staff?

Are there ways to increase income other than increasing the number of bodies? Do you need to figure out how to level the peaks and valleys of your business cycle? Do you have products that you could market? Could you offer other services? For example, if you are a trainer, do you also want to offer to be a keynoter at conferences? Or perhaps it is simply time to increase the fee you charge.

Think long and hard about this step. Once you change the makeup of your business, it will never be the same. You have dozens of options and combinations of options to consider. For example, when I decided that I wanted a "partner" in my business, we sat down and came up with the following list of possibilities for the business configuration:

- I own; you're employed.

- You own (buy me out); I'm employed.

- Equal partnership.

- Unequal partnership.

- I own the primary business; you own a subsidiary.

- We both own the primary business (equally or unequally); I own a related subsidiary.

- We create a franchise arrangement.

- You start your own business; we share overhead.

We were creative and tried to identify all the possibilities. You should do the same. Think hard and long; do all your homework; and talk to others who have done what you are thinking about doing before you make the move to grow. If growth is still on your mind, this chapter presents several options for you to consider.

ADDING PEOPLE

Because increasing the number of people is usually the first thing people think about when the issue of growth comes up, let's begin there.

Should You Hire Staff?

Beth was the first person I hired. I hired her part-time to be in my office when I wasn't in to answer the telephone. This was in the early years of answering machines and voice mail. An answering machine was a dead giveaway that you were new to the business and probably working off your kitchen table. In the early 1980s working from your home was not regarded as professional.

After I hired Beth, things started to snowball. I hired Beth for her telephone voice. I knew she would be great with clients. In addition to having a great voice, Beth also loved computers. She immediately started to do some of my word processing. That freed me up for more billable days. I took on more clients with more sophisticated needs. Therefore, we needed a better computer and a copying machine.

To pay for the new equipment, I started to take on larger projects. I was unable to provide the highest quality services by myself, so I started to hire other consultants. Beth could no longer keep up with the demands of additional clients, so we hired additional administrative staff for support. Of course that meant we needed more computers and a larger office. To pay for the additional equipment and . . . well, you get the idea.

Once you begin to hire staff, have a clear plan in place for exactly how much growth you desire and how you will fund this growth. I have read that a consulting firm must have seven or eight people before it truly turns a profit, provides the same flexibility an independent consultant has, and is worth the effort and investment. I have no data to back this law of diminishing returns, but I can tell you that I've been through it and I agree.

Advantages. The greatest advantage to hiring staff members is that they will be a part of your organization. Clients will see that you are growing. Some clients will be impressed with the number of employees that you have. I am asked on a regular basis, "How many employees do you have?" I have noticed that clients' interest levels rise in direct proportion with the number of employees we have.

A larger staff affords you the luxury of pursuing larger, more complex projects, and it is usually easier to manage several large projects than many small projects.

As staff members become a permanent part of your organization, you will become familiar with their talents and limitations. That means you will be able to more knowledgeably match them to the project, the client, or the industry.

Disadvantages. The greatest disadvantage of hiring staff is the ongoing payroll commitment. When our company was at its peak, I thought about how many people, roofs, tires, braces, and dogs were dependent on the success of the company.

More administrative tasks are required. As soon as you hire one person, you become an employer and the paperwork mounts: You need unemployment insurance, new federal and state tax configurations, an "office" where they can work, and a dozen other employee-related items.

One of the greatest disadvantages is one that you might think is an advantage: If there are other people in the organization, they can do more of the client face-to-face work and you can do more marketing. Wrong! It has been my experience that clients will want you to do the work. You have the reputation, and it's your name on the door. No matter what you do, clients will still want you. The only way to keep all the demands from falling on you is for the consultants in your organization to generate their own work. They need to make face-to-face contact with clients and also do their own marketing.

So if having additional consultants on staff was your solution to freeing yourself up from the grind of billing, go back to the drawing board. Unfortunately, it won't happen.

No matter what you do,
clients will still want you.

Exhibit 8.1 explores additional advantages and disadvantages. If you are considering hiring employees, take time to add your own thoughts under each item. When you have finished, go back and look at what you have written. Which side appears to be the stronger for you?

Should You Enlist a Partner?

I had a partner for five years and I would do it again if I could find another exactly like him. We were alike in some respects and very different in others. We communicated well, trusted one another completely, made decisions effectively, and complimented one another's skills. I've heard it said that taking on a partner is more like a marriage than marriage itself. So the choice of who to partner with is not a simple one.

According to small business owners, the single biggest mistake entrepreneurs make is choosing a partner too casually. A trial relationship can be established to explore the likelihood of a successful permanent one. I highly recommend an arrangement that allows you and your potential partner to work together for six to twelve months before making the relationship permanent.

Taking on a partner is more like
a marriage than marriage itself.

How to configure your partnership is a second concern. We decided that although we were going to be partners, it made more sense for us to incorporate legally as a subchapter-S corporation. (Chapter Four described the advantages of this legal entity.) We also decided that because I had more equity and eight years

	Exhibit 8.1. Building a Firm.	

Advantages	Disadvantages
Increased ability to serve more clients	Increased time necessary to educate new employees
Increased availability and types of services	Increased time in managing others could decrease time to serve clients
Increased earning base	Increased overhead
Security of backup in emergency	May invest time in those who will leave and compete with me
Spread my philosophy and increase name recognition	May have different values

in the company, I would maintain slightly more than half of the ownership. We agreed that we would draw the same salary after the partnership was formed. The split of dividends, of course, is governed by law. We would each receive an amount proportionate to the percentage of ownership.

Prior to becoming a partnership, my partner and I agreed that he would work for at least one year at a reduced salary. The salary not taken was his way of buying into the company. We established several other parameters. One was that, in addition to working for a year, he needed to show that he was generating an equal amount of work.

Often, dividing responsibilities and roles is the most difficult task. If you can be as lucky as I was, you can have roles and titles that clearly define the responsibilities. For example, a founding partner can focus on work with major clients and maintain the corporate vision, while a managing partner can manage the daily operation of the company, including taking over responsibility for sales and profitability. In our case, we were separated geographically: My office was in Wisconsin and his office was in Virginia. Each of the offices was responsible for different aspects of the business, for example, invoicing clients, bookkeeping, or producing client materials. Each of us had responsibility for an office.

Exhibit 8.2 is a discussion generator for checking partner compatibility. Each partner completes the questionnaire. At least half a day should be set aside to discuss both partners' responses. The discussion will uncover concerns and issues that could create problems within the partnership. Take care of them before a legal entity is formed.

Advantages. Consulting is a lonely business. Often the thought of having a partner seems like the perfect answer. There would be someone to bounce ideas off (consultants like to bounce ideas) and someone to cover for you if you were ill.

A partnership broadens your business capabilities, expertise, skills, and experience. This is one reason for partnering with someone who is unlike you—someone who complements what you bring to the business.

A partnership sends a message to the world that you believe the person you have elected to partner with is at least your equal. This is important if your present clients are to accept the person as a qualified substitute for you.

From a business perspective, there is someone to share the responsibilities or the cost of doing business—someone with whom to share the decision making.

💾 Exhibit 8.2. Partnerability.

Each potential partner completes this questionnaire. Set aside at least one-half day to discuss your responses.

Rate each item on a 1 through 7 scale with 1 being low and 7 being high.

| | | Low | | | | | | High |

1. The importance of my title 1 2 3 4 5 6 7
   My ideal title would be. . . .

2. The importance of salary 1 2 3 4 5 6 7
   My ideal salary would be. . . .

3. The importance of responsibilities 1 2 3 4 5 6 7
   The responsibilities I want are. . . .

   The responsibilities I do not want are. . . .

4. My commitment to this partnership 1 2 3 4 5 6 7
   Because. . . .

5. My willingness to challenge you 1 2 3 4 5 6 7
   Because. . . .

6. My level of trust with you 1 2 3 4 5 6 7
   Because. . . .

7. My willingness to take risks 1 2 3 4 5 6 7
   Examples are. . . .

8. The strengths I bring to this partnership are. . . .

9. The liabilities I bring to this partnership are. . . .

10. My five-year vision for this partnership is. . . .

11. My "must have's" or things I will not budge on are. . . .

12. My philosophy about travel expenses is. . . .

13. My philosophy about quality of work is. . . .

Disadvantages. The greatest disadvantage to having a partner was already listed as an advantage. You must share the decision making with someone! Depending on your agreement, each of you will probably need to check with the other before making a move. If you like independence and not having to ask permission to do something, shared decision making could get in the way of your relationship. In addition, it may take more time to make decisions.

You will need to share resources. This can be a concern, especially if one of the partners is either generating or billing a greater proportion than the other.

Should You Consider a Practice?

I think of a *practice* as having one key person (you) with others on staff in assisting roles and a *firm* as having numerous people who can do the same thing (many you's!), plus support staff (receptionists, administrative assistants, or word processors).

Advantages. The greatest advantage of a practice is having dedicated support. Someone is there to help with the ordering, scheduling, typing, copying, cleaning, filing, billing, packing, and the dozens of other things that need to be done. Someone is available to pick up the slack and share the administrative stress. If you're on the road and need something, someone is available who can fax or mail it to you.

Disadvantages. The greatest disadvantage of a practice is having someone on payroll who is not billable and cannot generate income. This means that you are working to support two people. If you decide to hire someone, make sure that it is worth your while. Will the person free up enough of your time so that you can easily make three times the individual's salary? If not, it is not a worthwhile pursuit.

Do You Want to Hire Subcontractors?

If you accept a project that is too big for you to handle alone, you may choose to hire subcontractors. It is an excellent idea from a tax perspective because you can add people on a temporary basis.

Subcontracting is on the increase. In addition to being helpful for large projects, the arrangement allows consultants to tap into one another's expertise. This allows you to seek projects for which you may not have all the qualifications.

Although I prefer to work on a handshake, if you have a large project for which you will use multiple subcontractors, we recommend that you use a subcontractor agreement. The more people involved, the higher the chance for mistakes, misunderstandings, and disagreements. An example of a subcontractor agreement can be found in Exhibit 8.3. In addition, the subcontractor expense record in Exhibit 8.4 can be adapted for your use.

┌───┐

💾 **Exhibit 8.3. Subcontractor Agreement.**

AGREEMENT

Whereas ebb associates inc, Box 657, Portage, WI 53901, has entered into a contract with the Client to provide materials and facilitation for a series of team-building sessions entitled "Building Your Team" (which shall be described as "sessions"); and whereas _____
(Facilitator) desires to and ebb associates desires to have Facilitator facilitate these team-building sessions; therefore, in consideration of the premises hereof, ebb associates and Facilitator hereby agree to the following terms and conditions:

I. Statement of Work

   The Facilitator shall use the materials provided by ebb associates to facilitate the sessions for the Client at the locations and dates to be determined by Client.

II. Facilitator

   Facilitator agrees to the following:

   A. Facilitate the sessions using the material provided by ebb associates in a manner that ensures consistency of content, detail, and method of presentation.
   B. Contact the Client team leaders before each session to ensure that content addresses unique team issues. The Facilitator will customize the session for each team. The Facilitator will verify all unusual requests from the teams with ebb associates.
   C. Become familiar with the nature of the Client's business, team needs, and environment. This includes reading the Client's strategic plan.
   D. Distribute and collect Client Evaluations at the conclusion of each on-site segment. All evaluations shall be mailed to ebb associates.
   E. Summarize in writing the results of the Client session using the Facilitator Evaluation as a guide at the conclusion of the facilitation. Write a brief report describing the session and relevant information collected during group discussions, including any significant events that the Facilitator considered either supportive of or detrimental to the success of the session and the ability of the team to be successful. Include comments about the logistics, the facility, appropriateness of the training for the actual audience, and any other noteworthy considerations.
   F. Mail the invoice, expense records and evaluations as appropriate within fifteen working days after each on-site segment.

└───┘

III. ebb associates

ebb associates agrees that it will:

A. Coordinate the schedule of training dates and locations with Client.
B. Perform final design, editing, proofing, printing, and preparation of the session materials for submission to Client.
C. Provide a Facilitator Manual and materials required to deliver the sessions.
D. Work with Client to ship participant materials to the training site.

IV. Period of Performance

A. The initial period of performance shall begin after award of the Client contract and extend through September 30, 1999.
B. Potential session numbers and dates for delivery are outlined in Exhibit 1 and are made a part of this contract. Client and ebb associates may request a change or cancel any of the dates set forth in Exhibit 1. The rescheduling of any such changes will be by mutual agreement of all parties. ebb associates and Client will be obligated only to pay for services provided.
C. Facilitator cannot be guaranteed a minimum number of billable days.

V. Facilitator Remuneration

A. For providing services for the session, ebb associates will pay the Facilitator eight hundred dollars ($800.00) for each day of facilitation. Payment of fees will be made only if Facilitator submits an invoice and expense record to ebb associates and after full payment is made by Client for said expenses. In no event, however, will Client reimburse at a rate higher than allowed by Joint Travel Regulations summarized in Exhibit 3.

VI. Billing Instructions

A. Submit your invoice, including the following information: Name, address, Social Security Number or Employer Identification Number, dates of facilitation, session number, fee at $800.00 per day, and total travel costs.
B. Invoices shall be submitted in original and two copies to:

Beth Drake
ebb associates, inc.
Box 657
Portage, WI 53901

🖫 Exhibit 8.3. Subcontractor Agreement, Cont'd.

VII. Copyrights and Other Rights

   A. All written materials provided by the Facilitator in the session shall be appropriately documented as to their original source (author).

   B. Unless Facilitator gives ebb associates written notice in advance that any part of Facilitator's contribution to the session is not or would not be Facilitator's original work and unless ebb associates approves in writing the use of any material that is not original, Facilitator hereby warrants that Facilitator's contribution to the session shall be Facilitator's original work and shall not infringe on the copyright or other property rights of any person, business, or corporation.

VIII. Miscellaneous Provisions

   A. The parties understand and agree that all provisions of this Agreement and all rights and obligations arising hereunder are conditioned and contingent on execution and parallel performance of the Client Contract, including performance of each corresponding provision in the Client Contract.

   B. A specific waiver by ebb associates or Facilitator of any provision of this Agreement on any particular occasion for any reason will not be deemed to be a basis for any automatic waiver of the same or any other provision hereof in the future.

   C. This Agreement shall not be deemed to create an employment relationship, a partnership, or joint venture and shall be interpreted according to the laws of the state of Wisconsin.

   D. Facilitator agrees that all requests for training and consulting services to be performed by Facilitator made by Client subsequent to this Agreement shall be scheduled and invoiced through ebb associates.

   E. This Agreement may be modified only in writing and with the consent of both parties. It is intended to bind only the parties hereto and their corporate successors and may not be assigned by either party without the express written consent of the other.

   F. This document contains the entire agreement between the parties and embodies all the terms of any prior agreements, understandings or representations, whether oral or written.

_____   _____

_____   _____

(signature)   (date)   (signature)   (date)

By: _____   By: _____

Title: _____   Title: _____

💾 Exhibit 8.4. Subcontractor Expense Record.

Contract _____   Invoice # _____

                                     Invoice Date _____

Consultant Name _____

Session Number and Location _____ Dates _____

Team _____ Number of Team Members _____ Billable Days _____

Travel Costs   *To be completed by Facilitator. Attach receipts for all (*) items.*

Airfare*/Train*/other... $_____

Rental Car* $_____   Gasoline* $_____ ....Total $_____

__/__/__ Taxi*/Shuttle* from _____ airport to hotel ...... $_____

__/__/__ Taxi*/Shuttle* from session to _____ airport .... $_____

Meals* (itemize) .... $_____

Hotel* .... $_____

Airport parking* .... $_____

Local Privately Owned Vehicle # miles _____ × $.35/mile or

    Taxi* from residence to airport .... $_____

Local Privately Owned Vehicle # miles _____ × $.35/mile or

    Taxi* from airport to residence .... $_____

                                     Total Travel Costs $_____

Session Costs *This section to be completed by ebb associates inc*

Facilitation fee $_____

Other $_____

(explain)

                                     Total Session Costs $_____

                     Total (Travel and Session Costs) $_____

Advantages. Subcontractors can be hired on a per-project basis. That means that there will be no ongoing payroll expense. You will not be required to withhold income taxes or pay any share of their Social Security or Medicare taxes. Generally, you will hire people who are skilled and professional. Subcontractors increase your flexibility, as you are able to hire the talent you need on a project-by-project basis.

Because they are independent, they know how important it is to produce high-quality work. They will work hard to satisfy your needs because it could lead to repeat work for them. They also require less administrative overhead. Your only obligation is to send completed 1099 forms to them by the last day of January.

Disadvantages. The greatest disadvantage is actually only a potential one. The Internal Revenue Service has adopted twenty common-law rules for differentiating between an independent contractor and an employee. The rules cover things such as whether you have the right to direct the person's work; whether you supply the person with tools and a place to work; whether you establish the hours of work; and whether you have a continuing relationship with the individual. Even if you have studied the guidelines and are complying with the law, the Internal Revenue Service could tie you up in an investigation for months. As an independent consultant, you can imagine what this might do to your business.

Subcontractors are not always available when you need them, and because they most likely substitute for other consultants, they will not know your projects well and may not understand your consulting preferences. This means that you may need to spend almost as much time bringing them up to speed for a project as if you did it yourself. You can only hope that the investment of time will have a payback in the future.

Subcontractors may also become your competitors. Ethically, subcontractors represent your company when they work for you. In addition, they are not supposed to discuss their own business nor are they to market themselves to your clients while on your project. Even if they do not, your client may discover the arrangement and may want to hire them directly to save money. This can be uncomfortable for everyone, especially you.

Can You Use Graduate Students?

University graduate students may be hired as interns for project work under arrangements similar to those of subcontractors, but you must still follow all IRS guidelines. You could also hire them as part-time employees, in which case you provide a payroll for them.

On occasion you may be able to locate a student who will work for credit only. If you have a thriving practice that provides an opportunity for learning to occur, this may be an option you should check into. Call your local campus to learn about your options. Call at least the business and communication departments. There may be other specialty departments to call also.

Advantages. Graduate students usually are interested in the experience more than the salary. That means that you can find lots of talent at a very good price.

You can complete projects that you have been unable to tackle in the past due to a lack of time. For example, you may assign a student to one specific project, such as developing a new seminar based on materials you have collected.

Disadvantages. The greatest disadvantage is that graduate students usually lack experience. They may have lots of knowledge, but not the practical hands-on experience that your clients expect. Even if they work as support staff, they may have little experience with running a copy machine, creating computer graphics, or answering a telephone.

University students are generally short-term employees. That means that you will not often have them for more than a school year—and usually for just a semester.

Due to class schedules, they may not be available when you need them the most. Sure as heck, they will have a big exam scheduled when you have a major project due for your best client.

GROWING WITHOUT INCREASING PAYROLL

As soon as you hire your first employee, you change the complexity of your business. You no longer have choices about where, when, and how much you will work. You now have a responsibility to another human being. Before you take that big step, consider growing without employees. How can you increase profits and yet maintain your practice as a sole employee? First, consider using your local temporary services to help you out on occasion. Second, try several configurations involving other consultants: Subcontracting for or collaborating with another consultant; joining a joint venture; offering other related services; or selling products that are related to your consulting work.

As soon as you hire your first employee,
you change the complexity of your business.

These are all viable options. Consider the advantages and disadvantages of each.

Could a Temporary Service Meet Your Needs?

One of the fastest growing industries in the nation is temporary services. Corporate America is outsourcing almost every kind of job. We use temporary services when we have repetitive tasks or simple processes to complete. Temporary services are useful when we have huge mailings (envelope stuffing, stamping, labeling) or for a large amount of word processing or copying.

We find temporary employees to be especially helpful when everyone in the company is busy with a huge project and we need someone to serve as a receptionist.

Advantages. Temporary services can provide the specific skills necessary for repeat work. It is a reasonable price for short-term prequalified support. If you are in a bind, temps can fill in at the last minute.

Disadvantages. The disadvantage of temporary employees is that the individuals have to be trained each time you are sent someone new. It is highly unlikely that you will be able to use the same person more than twice. If the person is good, he or she will be offered a permanent position.

Another disadvantage is that you will not always have the best person from the agency if there were many requests ahead of yours. Also, no matter how clearly you define the task, the person who shows up may not be able to live up to your standards of quality.

Do You Want to Subcontract?

You could become a subcontractor for another firm, offering your services directly or perhaps completing design and development behind the scenes. Remember that, as a subcontractor, you must be seen by the client as an employee of the firm for which you are doing the work. Many consultants' egos will not allow them to do that.

Advantages. As a subcontractor, you could continue to run your own business while subcontracting with others. This provides an opportunity for you to fill in the gaps when you don't have billable work. If you have been offered a long-term project, it could provide a steady income.

A big advantage is that you will be able to work for or with other professionals. This will certainly give you experience and knowledge that you might not acquire any other way.

Disadvantages. The greatest disadvantage to subcontracting is that you will most likely make about one-third of your daily fee. It is possible that you may need to turn down a full-paying project to fulfill your subcontracting responsibility.

You may have a difficult time working under someone else's business name—especially if you have had your own consulting business for any length of time. As stated earlier, we consultants typically have healthy egos that may create dissonance within ourselves.

Have You Considered a Joint Venture?

Some use the term "virtual partners" to describe a temporary arrangement, usually aimed at completing one project at a time. The parties involved are usually separated geographically, but that is not a requirement. The partners in the joint venture may work under a name that represents the group. That name may remain while partners may come and go, depending on the project.

Typically no legal agreements are made. However, you should not become involved in a joint venture without some written agreement among all parties. This will save you time and energy should something negative occur.

Advantages. A joint venture provides a temporary arrangement. This allows you to work with others on an experimental basis. It allows you time to determine if you would like to create a more permanent arrangement with some or all of these individuals.

The individuals have a shared responsibility for the outcome of the project, for completing the work, and for the financial success of the project.

Disadvantages. Because the joint venture operates under a loosely drawn up agreement, it is likely that something will be forgotten. The temporary arrangement exacerbates the situation, as individuals in the venture may not be as dedicated to its success as if they were in for the long term.

One of the biggest disadvantages is that the decision-making process may become convoluted—especially if more than two people are involved.

Do You Want to Collaborate with Another Consultant?

A collaborative arrangement is a fashionable growth option. You may hear a number of terms such as "alliance" or "coalition" or "consortium" to describe a loosely formed arrangement of shared resources, clients, and decisions.

Although a collaborative agreement is similar to a joint venture, there are some key differences. A joint venture is project-oriented; a collaboration is relationship-oriented. Membership in a joint venture is temporary and ends when the project ends; a collaboration is a continuing relationship and is maintained whether or not there is a project.

Collaborating is similar to a partnership but has fewer legal ramifications. Sometimes consultants collaborate with one another as a way to determine if they would like to form a partnership or corporation. Although the consultants may have good intentions, using the arrangement for that purpose is rarely a good idea. The loose agreement between two collaborating consultants is not the same as truly working together under a legal description that encourages individuals to make the best of any situation.

Before becoming involved in a collaborative arrangement, scrutinize the other individual or individuals. Does the person's image reflect favorably on you? His or her values, ethics, expertise, experience, and reputation should be similar to yours.

Advantages. Some of the greatest advantages are for your clients. Collaborating with someone allows you to add services to those you presently offer. The collaboration means instant growth in your customers' eyes. Another advantage to your clients is that you will have backup if something should occur that prevents you from being available on a scheduled date.

Another advantage is that the collaborating parties have more for less. The collaboration allows two consultants to pool resources for efficiencies in marketing, product development, and other high-ticket items. In addition, it allows them to share support staff.

A collaboration also increases opportunities for you to learn from another professional.

Disadvantages. Time becomes one of the greatest problems in a collaborative effort. Joint activities usually take more preparation time than solo events because you must discuss and plan as a team. Sometimes the projects each party brings get in the way and limit the time for joint activities. It is difficult for the individuals to give up these projects, as they are loyal to their clients. In addition, the projects most likely bring in money. In the end, it becomes difficult to find time to generate collaborative efforts.

Lack of a legal agreement causes continued separation, which can prevent the collaborating parties from learning to work together. The logistics may cause problems if the individuals live a distance apart. If they rarely see one another, they may not find the time to begin to meld their businesses together. If your values clash and you are not working together, the collaboration is doomed.

As with most things, money can create problems. Because the collaborative arrangement keeps the individuals separate, they may not make final decisions about how much to charge, how to share revenues, how to determine required investments, and a host of other issues.

If the two individuals are working in the same field, there may be crossover of clients. If this creates a competitive situation, the collaborative arrangement will end.

Do You Want to Offer Other Services?

If you are a trainer, you might consider offering keynote addresses for conferences. Keep in mind that the two require very different skill sets. You could offer other services. For example, a computer consultant could teach evening computer classes. Consultants can also write newspaper or journal columns, write and sell articles, tutor college students in their professions, or create and sell subscriptions to a for-profit newsletter.

Before you decide to take on a new service, decide what effect, if any, it will have on your business image. You may decide that it will have a positive effect and will enhance your consulting business. On the other hand, you may decide that it will engulf your consulting business or give it an image that is detrimental.

Advantages. The advantages of offering other services is that you broaden your skills and capabilities. There is always the possibility that you may discover another career that you like even more than consulting!

Disadvantages. The greatest disadvantage is that you may spread yourself too thin, taking on too many different things. You may not focus well. You may also become so tied up in a new venture that you will not be available for a consulting project when it comes up.

Most other "regular" jobs, such as teaching at a college or writing a newspaper column, require you to meet a consistent schedule, for example, show up every Tuesday and Thursday to teach. This does not fit into the erratic schedule of a consultant. You will need to determine whether two different services can live together under the same hat.

Can You Expand into the Product Market?

If you have been in business for a number of years, you probably have enough potential products in your files to fill a small library: Questionnaires, activity pages, surveys, survey results, reading lists, topic papers, quotes, checklists, tests, quizzes, summary sheets, games, puzzles—books' worth of things you have used once. Could they become products to sell to clients?

The members of the National Speakers Association (NSA) are truly experts at turning their materials into products. They take the best quotes from their speeches and turn out planning guides, pins, T-shirts, plaques, posters, CDs, tapes, workbooks, newsletters, and special reports! They may sell such products in the back of the room or to the client who hands them out after the presentation.

As a consultant, you don't want to open a store, but surely there is one book among all your stacks and files. Turn your favorite workshop into a how-to book for managers. How about a collection of self-evaluations or ten activities that will improve [you name it]. An interesting phenomenon occurs after you are a published author (even if you self-publish). You become an "expert." This automatically gives you the authority to increase your fees!

How about taping your next presentation and selling it? You could arrange to have it both videotaped and audiotaped. Tapes have gained in popularity since people have less time to read books. Many listen to tapes in their cars during a long commute to work each day.

Product possibilities are endless. Before you jump up and run to put film in your video camera, think about distribution. Who will sell your products for you? You could approach some of the large training product catalogs or publishers. I do not recommend that you attempt to market your own products. It takes specific knowledge and special skills.

Advantages. The advantage of producing products is really two-fold. First, you have ways to make money while you sleep; you could be selling a tape on the other side of the world at the same time that you are consulting for a client in your own city.

Products may help to even out the dips in the uncertainty of consulting. Products can provide not only an additional revenue source, but a *steady* revenue source.

Second, your products keep your name out there. Not only are you making money from them, but they will serve as marketing tools as well.

Disadvantages. Products take time and an investment of cash to produce. Then you must distribute them and let people know that you have them for sale. Products won't do you much good sitting in your garage. You must put them into potential buyers' hands.

Again, this is something you should discuss with others who sell products to determine if it is a viable option for you to consider.

DOING EVERYTHING YOU CAN TO GROW YOUR CURRENT BUSINESS

Ask yourself whether you have done everything you can to grow the business you now have. Sometimes we are so busy we forget the basics of the business we are in.

Some Questions

The following questions will jog your thinking about what you may be able to do with what you have:

- Have you recently studied your numbers? Have you compared them with past data? Have you conducted a reality check with another consultant to determine if your expenses are in line? If your income is reasonable?

- Have you become overly dependent on one industry? Is it time to expand or at least to explore other industries?

- Have you expanded the coverage of your market area? Can you serve clients in the next state? On the other coast?

- Have you selected clients who hire you for the kind of projects you prefer? Who can provide repeat work? Who can pay the rate you charge?

- Have you evaluated your consulting rate? Is it time to increase it?

- Have you kept up with technological advances? Are you current with how they affect your work? Have you incorporated them into your projects appropriately?

- Have you built relationships with your clients? With other consultants?

Your answers to these questions may contain some interesting answers for growth.

Final Thoughts

How can you determine the best way to grow your business? First, define what you mean by "grow your business." Next, think about the kind of consulting you conduct and determine the pros and cons for each option. Third, narrow your choices down to three; then speak with consultants who have grown their businesses using these methods. Fourth, consider the implications for the bottom line, your time, and the added responsibility. Is it worth it?

One of the advantages of being a consultant is that there are so many other avenues open to you. As you consider all your options, take care that you do not trap yourself into a financial commitment that you cannot support. If you decide to add individuals to your present business entity, consider the responsibility you have added and how that will affect you and your present business.

The Ethics of the Business

*"Have the courage to say no. Have the courage to face the truth.
Do the right thing because it is right. These are the magic keys
to living your life with integrity."*

W. Clement Stone

One of our founding fathers, Thomas Jefferson, said, "In matters of principle, stand like a rock! In matters of taste, swim with the current!" As a consultant your principles are always on the line, and your principles contribute to the ethics of the profession. Perhaps Thomas Jefferson could easily tell the difference between a principle and a taste, but it's a bit more complicated in the consulting profession.

One consultant will say it is appropriate to charge the full per diem for expenses, even if it's not used, because the organization budgeted for that amount. A second consultant will say it is inappropriate to charge for what was not spent.

One consultant will justify varying the charges if a client cannot pay the full amount. A second consultant will say that is absolutely wrong. Anything can be justified and argued for with facts.

Jokes abound about consultants, such as the one about the consultant who is asked the time by a client. The consultant asks for the client's watch and then says,

"Before I give you my opinion, perhaps you could tell me what time you think it is." One of the best ways to ensure that consulting is not a joking matter is always to provide services in the most ethical manner, to build relationships with the highest level of integrity, and to run a business with the highest principles.

Your reputation as a consultant will be created by thousands of actions, but may be lost by only one. It is imperative that you always model your high standards with clients, other consultants, and the general public.

Your reputation as a consultant
will be created by thousands of actions,
but may be lost by only one.

This chapter focuses on ethics in the consulting field. It will address the ethics issue from three relationship perspectives: Consultant to client, consultant to consultant, and client to consultant.

We take a fairly hard stand with regard to ethics for two reasons. First, we believe that the consultant's reputation has been tarnished by past practices and that taking a tightly focused approach may help to polish it to a reputable shine. Second, and more importantly, is that the practices we espouse here are those that we follow and strongly believe are right.

If you intend to join the consulting ranks, support the profession by maintaining high ethical standards. You will benefit everyone associated with the profession.

CONSULTANT TO CLIENT

Let's first focus on the consultant's relationship with the client, because that's the one that probably concerns you the most at this time. We will discuss consultant to client ethics in two categories—delivery of services and business aspects.

Delivery of Services

Some pointers for delivery are given in the following paragraphs.

Deliver Only the Highest Quality Products and Services. You have been paid to produce the highest quality products and services, at a reasonable price, on time, every time. Provide quality first, last, and everything between.

Accept Only Projects for Which You Are Qualified. Ethically, you must be willing to turn down a job that is beyond your competence. This does not mean that you should not accept projects that are a stretch or during which you can learn something. However, you should be able to contribute significantly to the client.

Learn on Your Own Time. You will always need to learn something about the project or a new client, and there is often a hazy distinction about who is responsible for the investment. Our rule of thumb is that we will invest 5 percent of our time learning about our clients. That is, if we have a contract that is about twenty days in duration, we will spend at least one day learning about the client without charge.

Turn Down Projects That Are Inappropriate. If you are asked to do something that is inappropriate from any standpoint, say no. In the middle of the data-gathering step for a team-building session, I learned that the manager who had hired me actually wanted me to collect data that would support firing a specific individual.

Place the Client's Interest Ahead of Your Own. This means that you will not take advantage of your client in any way—large or small. At the large end of the continuum, if you overbid the project, do not charge the full amount. At the small end of the continuum, it means not to take a limo when a taxi will do. You are charged with monitoring your own performance, as these are usually things that may never be uncovered.

Be Willing to Say "I Don't Know." Consultants must feel comfortable responding honestly, even when the answer is "I don't know." Some consultants think that they look weak if they do not have all the answers. Being honest with a client will gain more respect than will "faking it."

Accept Only Work That You Can Manage with High Quality. Consulting is notorious for having peaks and valleys. Therefore, consultants become nervous in the valleys and take on more work than they can manage later. They may fall behind on deadlines or cut corners to meet everyone's needs.

Accept Only Work from Organizations You Respect. When you work for organizations that you do not respect or whose business purpose may undermine your own values, you are hurting your own reputation. Watch for clients who may not appreciate your high standards of consulting or who try to reduce your quality. An advantage of being a consultant is the ability to choose your work.

Hold All Confidential Information Close. Never divulge any proprietary information or information about your contract. Although it may not appear so, it could give some other company a competitive advantage.

Avoid All Conflict of Interest. If you have the potential to benefit personally from any information you gain, you should not accept the project. For example, if you know that you will be in competition with the client in the future, do not accept the project.

Create Your Clients' Independence. The goal of every consultant should be to go into organizations, complete the work, and leave the clients better able to take care of themselves. An ad for a seminar entitled "How To Build and Maintain Your Consulting Practice" appeared in several newspapers recently. I was appalled to see that it touted "How to build your client's dependency!" A few more ads like that and most consultants will not need to worry about their reputations!

Repay Any Loss You Cause the Client. Inform the client immediately when problems arise or errors occur. No matter what the error, if you are responsible, own up to it and take care of it. This is not only an ethical issue, but you may be held legally liable if anyone is hurt or if the business is damaged in any way as a result of your error.

Complete All Work Yourself. If you find yourself in a bind and unable to complete an assignment, go to the client before you turn the project over to someone else. There could be another solution. Perhaps the client can take on more responsibility or was hoping to delay the project but did not want to change the agreement. You will never know unless you ask.

Avoid Working with Competing Clients at the Same Time. Due to the sensitivity of information to which you may be exposed, it is likely that it could have negative consequences if shared with the competition, even inadvertently. We take this one step farther. Due to the size and nature of many of our contracts, we will not work with clients' direct competition for a full two years after our last contact with them.

Conduct Regular Self-Examination of Your Practice. During and after consulting engagements, assess your progress and results. Learn from the experience.

Continue to Provide Excellent Services That the Client May Never Comprehend. Someone will notice. Even if no one does, you know you did what was right. We conducted the same workshop for a large manufacturer for eighteen months. Near the end of the contract a participant said she signed up specifically to meet us. She was from accounts payable and said she wanted to see the only trainers who were not gouging the company on expenses!

Business Aspects

Some ways to be more businesslike are given in the following paragraphs.

Adhere to a Consistent Pricing Structure. If you followed our advice in Chapter Three to establish a fee structure and to stick with it, you have already created an ethical foundation for your business. We said there that you should identify a clear and consistent pricing structure for all of your clients. Your structure should clearly spell out any differences among clients, such as nonprofit groups or government agencies, different kinds of work, or where the work is completed. Be consistent.

I once hired a subcontractor with whom I needed to establish a daily rate. When I asked him what his daily rate was, his first response was $1,200 to $1,600. When I asked what constituted the difference, he could not give me a specific or measurable definition. Two weeks later, he came to me and proposed that I take 15 percent and he take 85 percent of some arbitrary daily fee. I responded that we all needed to try to give clients as much for their money as we could. He finally agreed to accept a fee that ranged from $850 for writing, data gathering, and phone interviews to $1,100 for on-site strategy development. The client was able to accomplish about 30 percent more for the same amount of money.

Charge for the Work That Needs to Be Done. It may be tempting to charge more just because you know the client has more in the budget. Don't do it. You will never feel good about it. Also, don't add on services that the client really does not need.

What if you have quoted an amount and the project actually takes less time and effort? It's your call. You can justify charging the full price or you can buy surprised respect from your client by charging for only what was required. A number of years ago our company returned money to a large firm. The company called us to say that there was no process for putting the returned fee back into the system!

Charge Only for Reasonable Expenses Actually Incurred. Expenses are petty little things that can easily lead to a distrustful relationship. The easiest way to deal with them is to build things such as telephone calls and express mail into your daily fee, so that you neither need to track them nor present them to your client for payment.

Travel expenses should always be charged at cost and verified with receipts. Do not exaggerate mileage and do not exceed reasonable expenses. The question you should ask yourself is "Would I spend this if I were at home?" For example, "Would I eat this lobster dinner if I were at home tonight?" If the answer is no, it is probably not a legitimate expense.

Double dipping, or charging two clients for the same trip, is one of the worst ways a consultant violates the trust between consultant and client.

Expenses are petty little things that can easily lead to a distrustful relationship.

Bottom Line. Your fee structure, your expense report, and how you deliver your product are all important aspects of building an ethically strong relationship with your client. The bottom line, however, is that the ethical overtones will be dependent on the personal and professional relationship between individuals.

How can you determine if you are doing everything possible to build this relationship? Ask your client. Discuss it. Your client may not be aware of your standards or what you do to maintain them. This kind of discussion will build respect for you.

CONSULTANT TO CONSULTANT: SUBCONTRACTING

Subcontracting is a special relationship. Some guidelines for subcontracting are given in the following paragraphs.

Subcontractors Shall Represent Themselves as a Part of the Primary Consultant's Organization. Most clients feel nervous when they believe a group of independents, a hodgepodge of consultants, will come in to work on their delicate problems. Thus it is important to present a united front. As a subcontractor you give up the right to represent your firm or to discuss it. You give up that right in exchange for steady work.

Subcontractors Shall Not Market to the Client. Even if the client approaches you, the client belongs to the primary consultant, who has invested in marketing to this particular client. Report any offers you receive to the primary consultant. Perhaps the two of you can work something out, such as one or the other of you providing the service and the other receiving a percentage of the fee. Some firms have their subcontractors sign noncompete agreements. We do not do that. We state what we believe is right and then trust the subcontractor to do the right thing. We believe that a client is not fair game for a subcontractor until at least two years past the final contract date.

Subcontractors Shall Not Speak for or Represent the Client. Subcontractors should not speak for the client in contractual matters, changes in the delivery, or anything else. The primary consultant must take care of all issues and questions. The subcontractor should never discuss money with the client.

Subcontractors Shall be Positive and Supportive. Subcontractors must support in word and deed the delivery of services. The subcontractor's responsibility is to enhance the primary's performance. This is sometimes difficult. Egos get in the way. One tries to outguess the other.

Primary Consultants Shall Clearly Identify All Issues of Pay, Time, and Expectations up Front. Be completely honest and candid. State doubts you may have about any aspect of the project, even if it has not been stated by the client and is only your gut feeling.

Primary Consultants Shall Keep Subcontractors Informed. Subcontractors are very similar to employees, and you have the same ethical responsibilities to let them know if you have any concerns about the original plan. For example, let a subcontractor know if a project will be extended or shortened.

CLIENT TO CONSULTANT

Although you have no control over your client's behavior, you should be aware of some of the things clients may do that can undermine your relationship with them. I'd like to believe that some clients simply do not know better. In that case it is our responsibility to educate them. If we all inform them of the affect any of their behaviors have on us, we will improve relationships for all consultants and clients.

In other cases, the client may have an agenda that does not meet your standards. Typically you would learn about this during the early stages of the relationship. Turn the project down and find something else.

Sometimes the client's agenda is not apparent until later in the project. You may see warning signs along the way. The client may have unrealistic expectations of you or may begin to withdraw commitment from parts of the project. Be honest and candid with the client to resolve your concerns. If the client will not move back on track you can either work within the boundaries you have been given or quit.

What unethical actions might you encounter? Here are a few. *Prior to contracting with you, the client:*

- Wants to "pick your brain."
- Offers you lower pay than you quoted in your proposal.
- Has asked for your proposal in order to have the minimum number of quotes, without any intention of giving you the job. (Many clients have no idea that it takes four to twenty hours to write a good proposal.)
- Requests samples of product from several consultants, then puts them together and develops his or her own program based on information that came from the consultants.
- Already has decided what the answer is to the problem.

During the project, the client:

- Fails to provide data and information as promised.
- Is slow to approve work.
- Is slow to approve invoices.
- Shifts gears in the middle of the project.
- Refuses to remove barriers for you, such as difficult staff.

- Ignores your recommendations.
- Presents your ideas to management without sharing the credit.
- Requests that you omit information from a report.

CODE OF ETHICS

Most professional associations that represent consultants, such as the Institute of Management Consultants, have codes of ethics. If you do not know what your association's code is, call the customer service line and ask that it be sent to you.

As an independent consultant you will establish your own code of ethics. You will develop a set of ethical standards that you choose to abide by as you do business. That is both a privilege and a responsibility. It is a privilege that you have been given. As an independent consultant you do not need to live by others' ethics. It is a responsibility that you must accept. As a consultant, you have the ability to increase the public's respect and trust for the consulting profession.

If you have the courage to face the truth and do what is right, you will always feel good about the services you provide and you will do what is best for the profession. Place a high value on your talents and your high-quality service. Think highly of yourself. Do not sell out on your integrity; do not negotiate your reputation away. As a consultant your principles are always in jeopardy. When your name is on the project, your reputation is on the line.

---

*When your name is on the project,
your reputation is on the line.*

Exude Professionalism

*"If we did all the things we are capable of,
we would literally astound ourselves."*

Thomas Edison

What does it take to be a true model of success and professionalism in the consulting world? Probably the same things that it takes to be a model professional in any vocation, whether it's ballet, football, chemistry, landscaping, teaching, or writing. I once read that most people achieve only a third of their potential. Successful professionals in any position achieve much more than a third of their potential because they work at it.

Most people achieve only a third of their potential.

- Professionals assess where they are compared with where they want to be or where their customers expect them to be.
- Professionals continue to learn. They realize the value of expanding their knowledge and skills and of keeping up with industry trends.

- Professionals balance their lives and their businesses. They know the value of rejuvenation and renewal. They make conscious choices about how to spend their lives.
- Professionals manage their time. They are busy people who have learned ways to invest their time in the things that count.
- Professionals give back. No one "makes it" without the help and support of many others. True professionals give back to the profession, the community, their families, and their friends.

MEASURING UP

Successful professionals step back and take stock of where they are and where they want to be. They determine some measure of success, drive a stake in the ground, and head for it.

The next few paragraphs will help you assess where you are as a consultant. Many ways exist for you to measure how well you are doing. The following consultant competencies can help you start thinking about what you stand for as a consultant, where you are, and where you want to be.

Competency 1: Professional Standards

Establish standards for yourself that are high enough to keep you on your consulting toes and position a bar that encourages continual reaching.

Guarantee that your services will be the highest quality your clients have ever experienced. If you have employees, help them understand how important quality is to your business reputation. Put quality and your clients ahead of everything else—including profitability. What kind of a remark is that?! Especially from someone who has just written a book telling you how to run a financially sound business!

Establish standards for yourself that are high enough to keep you on your consulting toes.

It may very well be one of the best pieces of business advice in this book. The project will end; your relationship will not. You will learn from pricing mistakes and you will not make them again. Poor quality service mistakes will follow you and your reputation for life. A project that goes in the red is a small price to pay for a lifetime reputation. You are only as good as your last client says you are.

Set your standards high and never compromise them. Our standard is: Quality: first, last, and everything in between.

Competency 2: Professional Awareness

Stay on top of the profession by having a clear understanding of consulting, its practices, and where it's going. This includes knowledge of the state-of-the-art practice as well as the fads of the day; knowledge of the industry and consulting gurus as well as their philosophies; and knowledge of the professional organizations, journals, and newsletters that can help you stay abreast of the field.

One of the best ways to stay in touch with the field is to be an active member of your professional association. I often hear consultants say they "can't afford the dues." They have it all wrong. They "can't afford not to join!" Your ability to keep up with the profession is dependent on staying in touch. It is an investment in *you*. If you won't invest in you, who will?

Whether you have chosen the Institute of Management Consultants, the American Society for Training and Development, or the Instructional Systems Association, do more than just write the check for your annual dues. At a minimum attend the organization's annual conference. Volunteering for a committee is also a great way to stay in touch with the profession. You will be involved in the work of the profession, communicating with other professionals, and working with colleagues in your profession. It's an enjoyable way to come up to speed!

---

*It is an investment in **you**.*
If you won't invest in you, who will?

Competency 3: Consulting Skills

Your ability to do the work is a basic requirement. A professional consultant knows the basics of the consulting process: Defining a business need, clarifying expectations and reaching agreement (contracting), gathering data, recommending options, and implementing change. Continue to learn techniques and strategies that move you from being an apprentice toward being a master consultant.

In addition to becoming an expert at the consulting process, you will need other skills such as problem solving, managing meetings, designing surveys and materials, team building, and facilitating.

Certification or accreditation is available in many fields as a way of learning and achieving a professional standing in your profession. The accreditation could be related to your profession, such as a Certified Public Accountant (CPA) or a Certified Electrical Engineer (CEE). It could also relate to your specific consulting area, such as a Certified Speaking Professional (CSP), a Registered Organizational Development Consultant (RODC), or a Certified Management Consultant (CMC).

Competency 4: Communication Skills

The skill that goes awry the most often in any situation is communication. Therefore, you are probably not surprised to see communication skills listed as a competency. Your abilities to listen, observe, identify, summarize, and report objective information are important for a productive working relationship with your client. Equally important are your abilities to persuade, offer empathy, solve problems, and coach others.

Authentic communication, or stating what you are experiencing in the moment, is in Peter Block's (1981) words, "the most powerful thing you can do to have the leverage you are looking for and to build client commitment." This statement indicates how important authenticity is to the client relationship. Authenticity means that you are able to express who you are and what you are feeling clearly without being inappropriately influenced by those around you. It is honesty, candor, and clarity, combined with sensitivity to others.

Each of these and many other communication skills are requirements for a successful consultant.

Competency 5: Professional Attitude

Attitudes are elusive. They cannot be measured nor clearly defined, but we all know they are there. A professional maintains a positive attitude under all circumstances, asking, "What's good about it?" when something goes wrong.

The professional consultant is self-confident, can cope with rejection, is open-minded and flexible, and believes in people. Professionals take responsibility for their actions and are accountable to their clients.

Your attitude about consulting will permeate everything you do. If you love the work, enjoy helping your clients, get a high from the challenge of difficult projects, and find consulting to be an outlet for you as a person, you have probably found your niche in life. In *The Consultant's Calling,* Geoffrey M. Bellman (1990), suggests that you, "Pursue this work as a personal calling, bringing who you are to what you do."

Love what you do. I am delighted that I stumbled into the consulting field twenty years ago. I love the work and it shows. I believe you should not get up and go to work in the morning; you should get up and go to play. I am fortunate because I am allowed to play every day—and in the process make a good living. Consulting offers a good income, but if you are only in it for the money, you may not succeed.

You should not get up and go to work in the morning; you should get up and go to play.

Competency 6: Business Development

Generating work provides the steady flow of projects essential to stay in business. You must know enough about sales and marketing to be able to analyze your present situation, clarify a marketing strategy, set measurable goals, and select marketing tactics to accomplish those goals.

You must know how to develop an annual marketing planning calendar and how to monitor your results. You will want to determine how to even out your work load and income. Your ability to sell yourself and your services is the competency that keeps you in business.

Competency 7: Business Management

Staying in business is less dependent on how good a consultant you are than on how well you run your business. To stay focused, refer to your business plan on a regular basis.

Take care of the details of managing your business. Selecting a team of professionals to assist you (banker, accountant, attorney); tracking expenses and projecting income; invoicing in a timely manner; studying your data to learn how well you are doing; developing contracts and proposals; understanding office technology, systems, and equipment; dealing with suppliers; managing your money; scheduling, informing, and tracking clients and projects; and a myriad of other details are required to run a business. You will need to attend to these details to stay in business.

Competency 8: Building Relationships

Whether you are with clients, other consultants, or your employees, your success as a consultant is directly related to your ability to build and maintain relationships.

As a consultant, you do not have a tangible product that delights your customer. You have a service—one that may at times be difficult to define. Your service is invisible to the human eye; if you are truly doing your job, someone else may actually take credit for what you do. This helps to explain why building relationships is imperative.

Your Competency Level

Set time aside each year to assess how you are doing as a professional consultant. Your future success is dependent on how well you are doing today. Exhibit 10.1 is a personal checkup to determine how you are doing.

You may also wish to assess yourself on each competency. Go back to each competency above and rate yourself on a 10-point scale. Think of a 1 as representing a "beginner" level and a 10 as representing a "master" level.

It is likely that you will be high in some competencies and lower in others. It is also likely that you may have been higher in some areas in the past than you are today. For example, several years ago you may have been highly involved in your professional organization, but more recently you have had little involvement and your reading may have dropped off a bit. Two years ago you may have rated yourself as a 9, but today you may rate yourself as a 3.

After you have completed your self-assessment, you will want to create a professional developmental plan. The next section will help you with that planning.

CONTINUING TO LEARN

You have an obligation to your clients to improve your knowledge and skills continually. The rapid changes in the world today can turn today's expert into tomorrow's dolt if the person fails to keep up. The professional identifies a developmental plan for continued growth. Let's consider several strategies.

▢ Exhibit 10.1. Personal Checkup: How Am I Doing?

Think about your skills and behaviors as a consultant and respond to the following:

When working with clients, do I:

1. Develop a positive working relationship?

2. Communicate candidly, completely, and in a timely way with all stakeholders?

3. Maintain focus on the effort?

4. Respect all confidential discussions, comments, and information?

5. Create candid discussions about client responsibility and role in the effort or project?

6. Avoid internal politics and maintain an open mind?

7. Respect the organization's limitations of time, budget, and other resources?

8. Encourage the client's independence?

9. Provide regular progress reports that clearly identify the benefits of my work?

10. Ask for feedback on how I am doing?

11. Regularly evaluate my competence?

12. Upgrade my skills and knowledge beyond just what is needed?

Attend Learning Events

At a minimum, attend your professional organization's annual conference. It may be expensive, but you owe it to your clients to invest in yourself. I can think of no more enjoyable way to learn than to go to a great location, meet new people, renew past acquaintances, and attend sessions in which presenters discuss new ideas and approaches. To top it off, you may very likely go home with a fistful of business cards belonging to potential clients.

You have an obligation
to your clients to improve your
knowledge and skills continually.

To get the most out of your attendance, be sure to network. Don't sit on the sidelines or retreat to your room during breaks. You will not gain all the value that you can. Instead, go where the action is. Be the first to say hello. Introduce yourself to others and be interested in who they are. Identify common interests and experiences. Trade business cards. If the person has asked you for something or if you want to follow up after the conference, jot a note on the back of the business card as a reminder.

Go back to school. You may not need an M.B.A., but courses at the graduate level are critical. Take courses in finance, marketing, human performance technology, or organizational change. Take a class to bring yourself up to speed in the area of technology.

Ask Others

Ask for feedback from others on a regular basis. Ask for it from friends, colleagues, and clients. I sometimes conduct an exit interview to ask clients what they liked about my work on the project and what they wish I had done differently.

Ask clients about their most pressing concerns. Although this is not related to you specifically, the learning may be fascinating, and this will enhance your relationship.

Join an Association or Group

Affiliation with a national professional association or group is critical to maintain your professional awareness. Through the group, you will be kept informed of learning events.

Sometimes a professional organization will provide a networking list, designed to provide you with contacts in your geographic location. If not, form your own network. Networking is one of the best ways to continue to learn or, at the very least, to learn what you ought to learn!

Study on Your Own

Reading is one of my favorite methods of learning. The suggested reading list at the back of this book is a place to begin if you are interested in learning more about the business of consulting.

If you have not yet read the two books I have referred to several times, you must put them on your immediate to-do list: *Flawless Consulting* by Peter Block and *The Consultant's Calling* by Geoffrey M. Bellman.

Subscribe to and read your professional journals. Read general business magazines such as *Fortune, Business Week,* or the *Harvard Business Review.* Read the same publications your clients read to keep yourself informed about the industry. Read the new, cutting-edge journals such as *Fast Company.*

Read your junk mail. You will learn what your competition is doing, how to write more effective marketing letters, and how to design brochures. Realize that you will observe and learn from both good and bad examples!

Listen to tapes while driving longer distances.

Identify Resources

Sign up for an on-line service. The World Wide Web is a dynamic source for professional development resources. Sites provide information as well as link you to other related sites.

Visit your local technology training organization. Check out the classes they offer and other available resources they can lend you.

Visit your local bookstore. Browse the shelves looking for trends in the industries you serve and business in general. Thumb through all new books about consulting to determine if they should be on your bookshelf.

Co-Consult or Train with Others

Consulting with a colleague is a unique way to learn from someone else in the profession. It allows you to observe someone else, elicit feedback, and learn from the experience of working together.

Invite colleagues to observe you during a consulting or training situation. Ask them to observe specific things. Sit down afterward and listen to everything your colleagues say. Ask for suggestions.

Create Mentoring Opportunities

Meet with other professionals to discuss trends in the consulting profession. Some consultants form small groups that meet on a regular basis to share ideas, discuss trends, and help one another.

Identify someone in the consulting field whom you would like as a mentor. Then ask the person if that would be possible. My mentor and I meet for breakfast four to six times each year. I pay for our meals. This has become the best $10 investment I've ever made. I'm investing in myself.

---

*Often it is what you learn **after** you know it all that counts!*

Develop coaches in your key client industries. This requires effort on your part, because you may not cross paths with these folks on a regular basis. For example, several years ago I found myself working with several utility regulatory bodies. I remembered that my cousin had a friend who held a management position in the same industry. I called my cousin and set up a meeting with her friend so that I could learn more. He became a good friend as well as a resource, and now he calls me for coaching!

Identify where the experts hang out. Then go there. Sometimes this is a related association or an informal group. More seasoned people and those with different experiences can offer you priceless advice.

Aspire to the Best of Your Knowledge

Your clients expect you to be on the leading edge, regardless of your field. You have an obligation to them and to yourself to learn and grow. Learning is an ongoing process, even if you are at the top of your profession. Often it is what you learn *after* you know it all that counts!

BALANCING YOUR LIFE AND YOUR BUSINESS

Many people I meet think of consulting as an exciting, high-powered career: Flying from coast to coast, meeting with publishers in San Francisco and executives in New York City, staying at the Madison in Washington or the Ritz Carlton in Dallas, eating at a bistro in Manhattan or a coffee shop in Seattle. I am paid well, dress well, land large contracts, hobnob with the influential and famous. But that's only the first layer.

My friends know what my life is really like: Up at 4 A.M. to catch a flight for a noon meeting, spending six hours in an airport because of delayed flights, calling to cancel dinner plans, and finally arriving home at midnight. It is also about eating poorly prepared restaurant food, writing proposals until the wee hours of the morning, and losing a contract due to a technicality. Most of all it is about long hours.

Although you have the freedom to set your own schedule, the truth is that the hours are long. Projects demand your immediate and sustained attention. When you are putting food on the table, you may find it easier to stay glued to the project than to break away. In today's fast-paced world, no one finds balance an easy task. It becomes even more difficult when you are dependent on the success of the project your family now expects you to hold at bay while you attend the annual family picnic in Pauquette Park.

Although you have the freedom to set your own schedule, the truth is that the hours are long.

One of the most challenging issues facing consultants today is achieving a balance between the competing priorities of balancing their lives and their businesses; balancing their families and their work.

Joel Gendelman (1995), author of *Consulting 101*, says, "I actually installed a lock that had to be opened with a key—a key that only my wife had. She opened my office in the morning and closed up shop before dinner. The rest of the time, my little company was closed."

How can you achieve balance? What can you do?

Identify the Imbalance

Identify the three things you value most in life. Write them down. Now scan your checkbook and calendar. Do your choices match the three things you value the most?

Next ask your spouse, a colleague, or friend what he or she believes you value the most. Did that person choose the three things you chose?

Now begin to make real choices. What do you need to do to demonstrate the value you place on the three things you chose?

Make Your Own Rules

A business takes creativity and energy, so draining yourself becomes counterproductive. Of course, sometimes you stay late or work a weekend simply to meet a deadline, but do not make that your standard way of working. Make up a rule that helps to put your business in perspective. Tell yourself "If it's not done by 6 P.M. it will wait until tomorrow."

Enjoy the Doing

Don't hurry through each project just to get to the next one. If you love what you do, you may be missing some of the fun! Much of the pleasure may be in the doing.

Take Time Off

It is very important to take a break from your business. Go on vacation, even if you just spend a week at home. Invigorate your mind, rejuvenate your body, sleep late, relax, and read something that has nothing to do with work.

Identify Other Interests

Join a book club. Learn golf. Try embroidery. Fly a kite. Collect something. Visit an antique store. Try hiking. Read catalogs. Learn to paint. Take a cooking class. Write poetry. Work crossword puzzles. Refurbish a classic car. Study your heritage. Go for walks. Develop your family tree. Write a letter. Plan a trip. Do it with your spouse, your children, or a friend.

Take Advantage of Being at Home

If you work from your home, find ways and times to get away from it all. Go for a walk at noon. Visit the gym a couple of times each week. Read the morning paper in your kitchen or eat lunch on the deck.

Issues of balance become more acute during transitions. Therefore, if you are planning to transition to consulting, plan the transition. Focus on all of the important areas of your life: Social, family, spiritual, business, education. Identify how the balance might shift initially, and determine how you want it to change and how soon.

To some extent the issue of balance in life is really one of time management. Don't mistake busy-ness for business. You must prioritize deliberately, based on what you want out of life. Add a few of the following consultant time-management tips to those you already use.

Don't mistake busy-ness for business.

MANAGING YOUR TIME

Time is the one thing we all have equally. We all have exactly twenty-four hours in every day. The truth is that we cannot save time. Time continues to march on no matter what you insist. You cannot save time, but you can shave time—shave time from some of the things you must do that are less enjoyable. As a consultant there are two primary areas in which you can shave time—running your business and planning your travel. Try some of the following to shave time from each of these areas.

Business Time Savers

Here are some of the ways I've found for saving some time for myself and for managing my business.

The Big Jobs. Work on several large projects rather than dozens of small projects. You invest a great deal of time moving from one client to another, getting up to speed, flying from one coast to the other, reminding yourself of all the personalities, and remembering names.

End-of-the-Year Tickler File. I keep an end-of-the-year tickler file for my accountant. It's labeled "Take to Stephanie" and reminds me of all the things that have occurred during the year that I need to remember for tax purposes, legal responsibilities, and personal desires. It's a guaranteed method to ensure that I have everything that I need when tax time comes and that I am not at the last minute rummaging through stacks of paper trying to locate an Internal Revenue Service notice or a question from my attorney.

Invoice Ease. Keep an invoice format on your computer for clients who will incur repeat billings. When it's time to bill them, just pull it up, fill in a new date and numbers, and print it.

Postcard Contact. Keep a bundle of postcards in your briefcase. When you are on a plane, stuck in a waiting room, or have a canceled appointment, you can pull them out. Use them to keep in touch with friends, colleagues, and clients.

File Tips. Develop a system that works for you. You must keep up on the filing so you can move through your office, but you also want to find what you filed! We use different colored files to distinguish what's inside: Blue for project files, yellow for office files, red for client resources, green for volunteer activities, etc. We have separate cabinets to separate resources from client work. Make smart choices for filing your work electronically as well.

Phone Time. Calls can interrupt your concentration. If you want to stay focused, accept or return phone calls at a specific time. If you have a number of calls to make, make them in sequence. If the person is not there, leave a time when you can be reached, "I'll be available from 10:00 to 12:00 today."

Travel Time Savers

Travel can be hectic, but I have developed some ways to reduce the hassle and gain time for other activities.

Cash Stash. I have become almost entirely dependent on my credit card. However, there are still some times when I need cash. I keep $25.50 in the plastic pouch of my Daytimer™. If I'm traveling and do not have enough cash in my wallet, this amount will allow me to take a cab, buy a snack from a street vendor, or buy almost anything else that I cannot purchase with a credit card. The two quarters are handy for making a local phone call or plugging a parking meter.

One Travel Agent. We use one travel agent. We get fabulous service from Ginger and her gang. They know our preferences for services and carriers. We fax information about our trips to them, identifying times, destinations, and anything special. They fax an itinerary back for our approval. They have all of our frequent traveler numbers and enter that information as well. In addition, they deliver our tickets to our door. You cannot beat service like that!

Double Trips. Use a trip to work with one client and visit another potential client. Add a mini vacation to a special location when working with a client. In this case you will, of course, pick up all additional expenses.

Your Travel Bag. If you travel a great deal, keep the basics packed. I have two of everything: Curling iron, hair dryer, makeup kit, toothbrush, and so on. When I return from a trip I replenish anything that I used or emptied, such as pantyhose, underwear, toothpaste, deodorant, or whatever. This ensures that you will never forget any of the basics and makes packing a breeze.

You will never *find* time for anything; if you want time you must *make* it. The following list is a reminder of time-management tips you have always known, but may not be practicing. Try them. They work.

---

*You will never **find** time for anything; if you want time you must **make** it.*

- Set your priorities first thing in the morning or the last thing at night for the next day.
- Do your top priorities first.
- Tackle large projects in stages.
- Identify your "best" times, that is, your best time for writing, best time to make telephone calls.
- Use your waiting and travel time productively: Make lists, listen to tapes, write a postcard, balance your checkbook.

- Carry 3 × 5 cards or a small notebook to write down ideas or reminders.
- Handle each piece of paper once.
- Have a place for everything.
- Set deadlines.
- Make decisions in a timely way. Indecision is a time thief. Not only does indecision waste time, but it creates worry, which can be so destructive that you may be tired before starting the day!
- Always ask, "Is this the best use of my time right now?"
- Set a schedule. Stick to your schedule.
- Take short breaks often.
- Have something to do when you are put on hold.

Exhibit 10.2 is a time-management log. Although keeping the log is not a way to manage your time better, you must collect data to find out where you are spending your time. The log is divided into quarter-hour increments. Track your time for two weeks to obtain a good sample. Diligently record what you were doing and for how long. Next, determine your key job categories. You might include marketing, consulting, administration, and professional development. Add a category for personal things.

After you have the data, determine what percentage of your time you spent in each category over the two-week period. Is that what you expected? Did you spend too much time in some categories? Too little in others? What can you do to change?

Exhibits 10.3 and 10.4 are two time-management tools that I cannot live without! The calendar shows me my entire month at a glance. There is room for almost everything that I need to keep myself organized. In addition to meetings and appointments, I have room to include the individual's telephone number, departing and arrival times for my flights, important monthly reminders, and social engagements. I need to see the full month to have a feel for how things flow from day to day and week to week.

The session planner has all the details for a successful event. I start it the day the project is scheduled. It initially serves as a memory jogger to ask all the right questions. Later it helps our staff to know what needs to be prepared and packed. On-site it provides all the information about where to go for the consultant. It also tells staff how to get in touch with the consultant. Both of these forms have been

💾 Exhibit 10.2. Time-Management Log.

Name: _____   Date: _____

Hour	15-Minute Intervals				Daily Summaries
12:00 am					
1:00 am					List task categories after each letter
2:00 am					code (i.e., meetings, telephone calls,
3:00 am					marketing, consulting, administra-
4:00 am					tion, planning, etc.). Then put the
5:00 am					corresponding letter into the block
6:00 am					that was dominated by each task.
7:00 am					Do not allow more than one hour
8:00 am					to pass before updating this log.
9:00 am					Multiply the number of blocks by
10:00 am					15 minutes to find out how much
11:00 am					time was spent on each task.
12:00 pm					
1:00 pm					

Code   Task   #   Total Time

A. _____ ___ × 15 = _____
B. _____ ___ × 15 = _____
C. _____ ___ × 15 = _____
D. _____ ___ × 15 = _____
E. _____ ___ × 15 = _____
F. _____ ___ × 15 = _____
G. _____ ___ × 15 = _____
H. _____ ___ × 15 = _____
I. _____ ___ × 15 = _____
J. _____ ___ × 15 = _____

Hour	15-Minute Intervals			
2:00 pm				
3:00 pm				
4:00 pm				
5:00 pm				
6:00 pm				
7:00 pm				
8:00 pm				
9:00 pm				
10:00 pm				
11:00 pm				

■ **Exhibit 10.3. Calendar.**

Month: _____   Year: _____

Sun	Mon	Tue	Wed	Thurs	Fri	Sat

🖫 Exhibit 10.4. Session Planner.

Date: _____ Company: _____

Topic: _____

Contact Person: _____ Phone Number: _____

Purchase Order: _____ Fee: _____

Speaker/Presenter/Consultant: _____

Time Held: _____ Number of Participants: _____

Where Held: Address: _____

Building: _____

Room: _____

Directions:

Travel: Hotel: _____

Daytime Phone: _____ Nighttime Phone: _____

Directions:

Equipment: ___ Flip Chart(s) and Markers   ___ VCR Player and Monitor

___ Slide Projector   ___ Video Camera (with zoom lens)

___ Computer LED   ___ Blank VCR Tapes

___ Overhead Markers   ___ Blank Transparencies

___ Overhead Projector and Screen

___ Other: _____

Room Configuration: _____

Confirmation with Company: [ ] By Phone   [ ] By Letter

[ ] Date   [ ] Number of Participants   [ ] Address/Location

[ ] Hotel Arrangements   [ ] Equipment Needs   [ ] Room Configuration

[ ] Consultant Arrival Time [ ] Purchase Order Number

Materials: Binders: [ ] Gray ebb   [ ] See-Thru   [ ] Other: _____

Folders: [ ] Gray   [ ] Other: _____

[ ] ebb Seal Sticker   [ ] ebb Business Cards

Unbound: [ ] 3-Hole Punch   [ ] Staple   [ ] Other: _____

Supplies: ___ Table Tents   ___ Name Tags   ___ Markers   ___ Trainer's Manual

[ ] Other: _____

Special Instructions:

worked and reworked until they work well for me. Rework them so that they help you manage your time.

Manage your time well—it is your most valuable resource. Guard it jealously. Once it is gone, you will never get it back.

Manage your time well—
it is your most valuable resource.

GIVING BACK

You have received assistance, advice, and ideas from others as you have advanced in your career. Now you are probably asking for more of the same as you consider a consulting career. You may feel as if you owe many people. How can you pay them back?

Do the same in return. It takes time to invest in others and you should always be ready to give back—give back to clients; give back to the profession; give back to your community; and give back to individuals.

Try some of these ideas:

- Mentor someone just entering the field.
- Volunteer your services to a social service organization.
- Volunteer services to a civic group.
- Volunteer to help a children's group.
- Serve on local government or civic boards.
- Provide pro bono work for a local nonprofit organization.
- Send a thank-you card.
- Volunteer to serve on a committee for your professional association.
- Volunteer to speak at your local professional chapter meeting.
- Speak at your local high school's career day.
- Start a scholarship fund.

If you're thinking about being a consultant, don't stop there. Be a respected, knowledgeable, well-balanced consultant! Be a successful consultant. Be a highly professional consultant. Be all the things that you are capable of being. Astound yourself!

Do You Still Want to Be a Consultant?

"Life is either a daring adventure, or nothing."

Helen Keller

The most important reason to become a consultant is because you want to do it. If you have reached this chapter and the disadvantages don't discourage you and the challenges excite you, you are ready to develop an action plan that will take you into the world of consulting.

This chapter provides an example of a week in the life of a consultant. It raises lifestyle issues that do not fit neatly into other chapters. One of the most salient reasons for becoming a consultant is that you can create the lifestyle you choose. Therefore, this chapter provides visioning exercises that will help you to clarify your future.

If you answer the chapter's title question with a "Yes!" an action plan is provided to begin the planning and execution of your consulting practice. It provides a structure to take you from "I *want* to be a consultant" to "*I am a consultant!*"

Finally, if you are not quite ready, this chapter's Fast Fifty exercise will start you thinking about what you can do next to move "closer to ready."

217

A WEEK IN A CONSULTANT'S LIFE

It is Saturday afternoon and I am completing this book on my laptop at home. I missed the deadline earlier this month and now Kathleen, my editor, has impressed on me that it is crucial to have this on her desk next week. I am several hours behind my original schedule today because I was on the telephone for three hours this morning speaking with a client and my co-facilitator for next week.

The most important reason
to become a consultant
is because you want to do it.

Although the book is not due for seven more days, I will leave tomorrow, Sunday, on the 5:10 P.M. flight to Washington, D.C., to work with a client. Therefore, I must complete this manuscript today—or tonight.

I could take the manuscript with me to Washington, but I have learned that if I do I will not work on it. Therefore, if I am not near completion, I will call my date for the evening and cancel our dinner plans. I don't always do this, but this book is a priority—Kathleen's.

If I look out my window I have a beautiful view of the lake, which is sometimes distracting and sometimes inspiring. If I look around my home office I see the stacks that represent eight major client projects I will complete over the next month.

If I look in my briefcase, I will see a full year's calendar printed on 8½"×11" paper, with the present month folded to the top. It is scribbled full of notations, phone numbers, meeting times, and locations. I also see about a dozen various colored files—each representing a different project.

There are eight blue files, each one representing a client project. Three are two-day team-building sessions, one to be conducted in San Diego, one to be conducted in Arlington, Virginia, and the third to be conducted in Seattle. Two blue folders represent two different divisions of one company for which I will facilitate separate year-end evaluations and planning for the coming year. The last three files represent three year-long projects with clients in Virginia, California, and New York.

As I scan them, I am reminded that there is a chunk of design work connected to one of the projects. I muse that those eight blue folders represent more work than I would have been expected to produce internally in a year. Politics, policies, meetings, and other things prevented me from being more productive in those settings.

There are two green folders, representing two volunteer projects. I am a member of the national nominating committee for my professional society. I will make about sixty telephone calls over the next six weeks recruiting board candidates. I will present a session entitled "Creativity and All That Jazz" in New Orleans for another professional organization's marketing conference.

There is one gray folder, representing a special project. I am the consulting editor for the Jossey-Bass/Pfeiffer *Annuals*. I am developing an aggressive acquisition strategy for the next publication.

The orange folder holds a proposal for which we are awaiting a response. I am carrying it with me in case the company calls and wants something clarified.

The yellow folder contains my expense sheet, last week's financial report, the year's income projections, and the monthly expense/budget sheet. These four pages, combined with my calendar, contain enough data for me to make a number of decisions.

I have also packed the latest issues of *Harvard Business Review, Training and Development,* an OD newsletter, and a copy of *The Leader of the Future.* These are all airplane reading.

Floating among the folders is a little black brochure advertising the Innovative Thinking Conference. My thought process is something like this: "I should go. The fee is too high—$2,800 plus airfare and lodging, but the line-up is great—John Kotter, Frances Hesselbein. I'm too busy. But I deserve a break. It's too late to plan anything around the trip. My favorite author, Charles Handy, is presenting. But I really should get those marketing letters out. I'll think about it on the plane."

Speaking of planes, my nylon ticket folder is in the front of my briefcase, bursting at the seams with the tickets for the next couple of weeks. It also holds my travel i.d. cards and a spare stash of business cards. My small wallet that holds everything I could ever need (I gave up carrying a purse fifteen years ago) is also tucked in the front of my briefcase.

I have several lovely leather briefcases, but I continue to use my black nylon Lands' End model. It is light and easy to swing on my shoulder as I drag two suitcases on wheels through airports from coast to coast.

As an added thought, I stuff a dozen catalogs (Lands' End, Bloomingdales, Gumps) in my briefcase (you can always stuff one more thing in it). I like travel. And I like flying. Really!

I like the hustle and bustle of busy airports. I like the takeoff; it gives me a surge of energy. I like the freedom to be unavailable so that I can read without interruption or distraction. I read books (fiction and nonfiction), catch up on my reading of professional journals, and shop. Shop? Yes. I love catalog shopping and find that flights are a great time to thumb through catalogs and rip out pages that picture gift ideas. Later I'll make final decisions about which items to purchase for others or for myself.

I need to plan for the week. I will work for the client three days. Monday and Tuesday I will lead a team-building session off-site. I will be on-site to set up by 6:30 A.M. for an 8 A.M. start and will return to my hotel room about 6 P.M. After reading and responding to the fax from my office, I will order room service and begin to compile data from the session and prep flip charts for Tuesday's session. I will also review my strategy for the session and refine my agenda for the next day.

Tuesday I will arrive about 7:15, as I have little to set up. I expect that at least one participant will arrive early to talk about the day before or my profession or almost anything. The session will end by 4:30 P.M., and it will take another half hour to pack up and to add notes so that my office staff will know what to do with some of the materials. I will probably have dinner with someone from the company that evening. It will be a late night—dinners with clients usually are.

Wednesday I will work with another department to assess their needs, begin to identify unnecessary or duplicate processes, and establish a plan for them to continue when I leave. This organization uses me in many capacities. I have worked with them on and off for six years. I know a great deal about their people and their business. Lunch will probably be planned before I arrive and brought to the room where we will be working.

I will fly home Wednesday evening, stop at the office for an hour to better prepare me for the next day, and arrive at my door shortly after midnight. Thursday morning I will pick up a cappuccino (with whipped cream and freshly ground nutmeg) and be at the office before 8 A.M. Thursday will be a catch-up day for me. I will return phone calls, proof proposals, finish old projects, start new projects, write letters, hand-write a half dozen notes to clients and colleagues, add my opinions about office issues that concern others, and just catch up on everything else. I will leave the office around 6 P.M., after making phone calls to the West Coast.

Friday I will stay home to work on projects that require more concentration. At noon I will go into the office for an hour or two. Mid-afternoon I will head for Madison (a one-hour drive) to have my hair cut and pick up some books I ordered at Border's. I will probably call a few colleagues to see if they would like to join me for dinner. Of course, I waited too long again and they will all probably have plans with other people who do not travel.

After reading these paragraphs you may have some questions. Let's tackle each of your potential questions, as each represents an aspect of the consultant's lifestyle that you may wish to consider before becoming a consultant.

- *Why is she writing a book and why isn't it her own priority?* Consultants write books as a marketing tool, to demonstrate their knowledge and expertise, and to share something with the rest of the world.

I write for the joy of writing. Unless you have a best seller, you will not make money from the book itself. Self-published authors claim that they do make money, but then you need to deal with distribution and other hassles I don't want. Because the book now has someone else's deadline, it is not fun. It is now Kathleen's priority, not mine. However, Kathleen is my customer and I will finish. Why do a book at all? Being published is equated with expertise for some. This allows you to charge a higher fee. I am already at the top of what I consider a fair client fee. I write for the joy of writing. As a consultant, you may write for other reasons.

- *Why can't she take her laptop and finish the book next week?* Consultants owe their clients their undivided attention when they are working for them.

When I work with a client I am completely absorbed by the work at hand. I rarely think about the other projects in my briefcase. I am focused completely on the client for whom I am working. It's difficult to go back to a hotel room after focusing for twelve hours on one client and switch gears to write a proposal or even a letter, let alone a book! The long hours require some down time. If you go out to dinner with a client, you can expect a late night.

- *Why did she spend three hours on the telephone on a Saturday and why is she traveling for business on Sunday?* Weekends may not always be free for a consultant. Saturday morning is often seen as a catch-up time for consultants.

I try to make myself available to all clients at any time. Everyone I work with is busy! It is frequently impossible to find a time when two of us can meet in person or by phone. Clients want to talk on weekends and evenings infrequently. Other consultants prefer to talk on weekends more often. The Sunday travel is my choice. If I travel on Monday I have lost another billable day. If I schedule a Monday-Tuesday assignment, I could still easily be available for a Thursday-Friday assignment if necessary. As a consultant you will need to determine how working or traveling will affect your weekends and your lifestyle. You will also want to consider how you will choose to balance being available to clients and still respecting your personal lifestyle.

- *How often does she cancel social plans for work?* Consultants do not work a typical workday or workweek and may need to switch social and work times around.

I rarely cancel social plans after I make them. However, I must admit that it takes a concerted effort to schedule social activities. I have to think about them a week in advance and put them on my calendar. When I arrive back in town on Friday evening, it is usually too late to plan for weekend activities. On the positive side, I have the option to build social time into my workweek. I do not need to ask anyone for permission to take an afternoon off for a haircut. I can add a day to my New York trip for shopping. I can browse in a bookstore on a Wednesday morning as long as I choose. As a consultant, you will have total freedom to set your own schedule.

- *How does the setting affect her work?* Consultants choose where they will work.

My surroundings affect my work greatly. I need the sun and water and a view when I am creating, developing, or designing something new. As a consultant you will be able to select where you want to live. As long as you are a short drive to an airport, you can live anywhere. If you decide you do not want overnight travel, you will need to live near your clients.

- *How often does she work at home? What are the benefits? What are the drawbacks?* Consultants can choose to have an office and work only there, choose to work out of their homes, or any combination of the two.

I complete any work that requires creative input in my home, where I have a separate room furnished with a desk, equipment, and supplies. My office, however, is better equipped, and most of my resources are there. In addition, I have staff at the office to support me when I experience a computer glitch or need assistance. These factors sometimes make it easier to work at the office. I have a fax machine in each location. I have a printer in each place. I travel about 70 percent of the time.

Of the remainder, I probably spend half at my office and half at home. You will need to determine how having an office in your home will affect your lifestyle. The benefit is that I have total privacy. The drawback is that I can easily be distracted by a half-dozen personal projects.

- *Why does she refer to the color of the folders?* Consultants are always on the go. They need to find ways to have an office-in-a-bag.

The colored folders display what I have to do at a glance: Blue for projects, green for volunteer work, and so on. The color coding also simplifies filing and retrieval. Other things that round out my office-in-a-bag include a miniature stapler, Post-it Notes™, paper, pens, highlighters, small scissors, an address and phone listing of key contacts, cash, comb, breath mints, lipstick, an extra pair of panty hose, spare frequent flyer coupons, and a throw-away rain poncho. I think you can imagine why I need each item. As a consultant, you will determine how much time you will live on the road, out of your car, or at home. In any case, know that you will be busier than you originally expected. Decide how that will affect your lifestyle and what you can do to prepare for it.

- *Why does she use a paper calendar rather than an electronic schedule?* Consultants are usually bouncing from project to project; they need to find ways to be organized.

I personally like to be able to pull my calendar out in a phone booth, the back of a taxi, or anyplace without plugging in a computer. I don't need my computer to be organized. I like my paper calendar. In addition, I have one calendar for both professional and social engagements. My friends are all over the United States, and I like to schedule visits with them in conjunction with my travel schedule. I like to see everything I'm doing in one month at the same time. On the other hand, technology allows you more flexibility than you could ever imagine. You will want to determine how technology will affect your lifestyle and what you must do to keep yourself organized. Do what works best for you.

- *Why does she refer to her volunteer work?* Consultants can be role models for giving back to the profession and their communities.

I volunteer because it is good for my soul. I like to volunteer. I did not get where I am without hundreds of generous people giving me something—a lead, a reference, an idea, time, encouragement, or a chance. Volunteering and helping others enter the field is my way of giving back to a profession that has given so much to me. Think about how some volunteer or pro bono work can fit into the lifestyle you are creating.

- *Why does she carry the financial information with her?* The financial data tells a consultant if the mortgage will be paid next month.

I carry it with me so that it is readily available if I need to make decisions. Besides, it really amounts to only four pieces of paper that are updated weekly or monthly. They are printed directly from the computer, and I toss old ones away as I receive updates. You will need to determine how you will be able to fit data analysis into a schedule that dictates that you will not always be at your desk.

- *What's significant about the reading materials?* Consultants typically read a lot to stay on top of the profession.

What is significant about my reading list is what is missing, more than what is there. Although I have a good selection of professional reading, I typically pack a good fiction book for balance. My not taking a fiction book signals that this is a busy month. As a consultant you must determine how you will keep up with all your reading.

- *Why can't she decide about attending the conference?* Consultants owe it to their clients to stay on top of things.

I know that and I know that I need to attend a conference like the one described. As you read, there are always issues and events that will tug at you. Every argument is viable. You must determine how you will make decisions like this one. The lifestyle you choose will be a factor to help determine which is more important: Feeding your brain or feeding your bank account; taking a break from work or catching up on work; capitalizing on an opportunity to hear leaders in the field or capitalizing on an opportunity to market to clients on your list.

- *Why the discussion about a briefcase, purse, and luggage?* Consultants have many things to juggle.

I try to simplify, simplify, simplify! That means ensuring that I have whatever I need wherever I go, but not one thing too many. Simplifying does not mean eliminating everything. If it rains and I don't have a poncho with me, I will need to scurry around solving a different problem. That's not simplifying. I keep a suitcase packed with all the basics; I avoid checking luggage to save time and to avoid the hassle of lost luggage. If I do need to check luggage, I always have what I need for the first twenty-four hours with me in my carry-on bag. I need wheels on my luggage so that I can cruise through airports and to a taxi without being dependent on a porter. You will want to look at the lifestyle you now lead to determine how consulting will add complexity or how it could simplify it. Ask yourself if you have the physical stamina for the rigorous travel that may be required.

- *Will she pack her laptop in her briefcase too?* Many consultants carry laptops in order to communicate by e-mail.

I am not a strong proponent of e-mail. I receive more junk mail there than in my mail box. People tend to address messages to many people because e-mail makes it so easy. I do not need to read 90 percent of the e-mail I receive. The greatest drawback of e-mail is that people believe that you will receive it, read it, and respond to it immediately! This is not the case. If I am with another client, I may not be able to get back to someone immediately. I do not want to drag my computer on every plane I board. I travel with my laptop if I need it for design or writing; otherwise it stays at home.

———————

The greatest drawback of e-mail is that people believe that you will receive it, read it, and respond to it immediately!

———————

- *What's all the fuss about airplanes?* A consultant's travel can take up time, reduce productivity, and affect his or her personal life.

It is not uncommon for me to visit both coasts in one month. I am on an airplane every month. Because I do not live near a hub, I change planes for every trip. One trip usually means four airplanes. Yes, I rack up frequent-flyer miles—over 2,000,000 and still counting. But the drawback that will affect your lifestyle is the difficulty in maintaining balance. Consider two simple things: food and exercise. You really must work hard to eat in a healthy way and exercise while on the road. How will you approach travel as it affects your lifestyle?

- *Why are the details of her schedule significant?* A consultant's schedule is usually hectic.

The week that I described is pretty typical. I don't try to get my week down to forty hours. I don't think I will ever try. I love what I do and I have created ways to build things other than work into my work schedule. Who do you know who can shop in New York City one week and in San Francisco the next? How many employees can take time off for a haircut or to browse a furniture store during the week? Who do you know who can work at home by choice? Who do you know who could take a stack of journals and sit next to a lake to catch up on his or her professional reading? Although I may have worked about seventy hours in addition to travel time in one week, I will have many opportunities to balance those hours. Your lifestyle could change dramatically based on schedule alone. Will you have your family's support for a dramatic change?

Your lifestyle is yours and yours alone. Decide what you want your lifestyle to be like as a consultant. Some visualization activities are given below to help you clarify what you want your consulting lifestyle to be like and to help you plant that lifestyle firmly in your mind so that you are more likely to create it.

VISUALIZING SUCCESS

A friend of mine was a high school state champion tennis player. Her coach required her to spend hours visualizing success. She visualized herself completing specific strokes perfectly. She visualized herself winning a match. She visualized herself as a champion. Coaches of many other sports use visualization as well. They ask athletes to close their eyes and visualize what the pass feels like leaving their hands, what the wind feels like against their faces, what the ball looks like going through the hoop, what the crack of the club against the ball sounds like.

You can do the same thing. You can be your own coach. Of course, before you do that you must have a clear picture of the kind of future you want. Turn to Exhibit 11.1. This exercise will help you determine how you want to live and work—how you want to spend your time. Find a quiet place—one where you are sure you will not be interrupted by a phone call, a visit, or a nagging chore. Take at least an hour to complete the exercise. Take more time if you can. Put it aside. Sleep on it. Feed your subconscious by thinking about it before you sleep. Then dream about it. Pull it out again and fill in more details. Now discuss it with your significant other. Make additions or deletions.

▣ Exhibit 11.1. Visualize Success.

Take a few minutes to imagine a successful future for yourself. Think in terms of three to five years. Describe your successful future.

Part I. Professional

1. Describe your professional goals. (What is your title? What do clients say about your work? What do your colleagues say about you?)

2. Describe your interactions with your clients. (What are you doing? Where are you doing it? How does it feel? To whom are you talking?)

3. Describe your work more thoroughly. (How many people are around you? What is their relationship to you? What work excites you?)

4. Describe the logistics more thoroughly. (How much do you travel? Where? For how long? Why? What does your office look like? Where is it? What is the view outside your office window?)

5. Describe the results of your work. (What honors or awards have you received? What is your annual salary? What profit does your business make? How much is in your retirement account? Your savings account?)

6. What other professional dreams do you have? (What other professions? What other work?)

Part II. Personal

1. Describe your personal goals. (What are you doing? What percentage of your time is spent pursuing personal goals? Where are you? With whom?)

2. Describe your interactions with family and friends. (What clubs have you joined? What vacations have you taken? What are you doing? Where? With whom? How does it feel?)

3. What do you do when you are alone? (What are you reading? What are your daydreams? Where are you?)

4. What are you learning? (Are you taking classes? Did you earn an advanced degree? Where? How? Why?)

5. What personal skills have you acquired? (What hobbies are you trying? What sports are you participating in? With whom? How often?)

6. Describe the logistics of your personal life. (Where do you live? What is your living space like? What kind of car do you drive? How are mundane chores completed?)

Place your visualization exercise in a safe place. Perhaps in your end-of-the-year tickler file or perhaps you want to give your dream one year. Make an appointment with yourself one year from now to review your desires. Realize that you may not have achieved all that you identified. Realize also that some things may have changed. In any event, you will most likely learn much about yourself and what is important to you.

Create a "successful future" file to keep your ideal future in front of you. You may wish to place your Visualize Success exercise in the folder. However, because pictures speak louder than words, shout your future by collecting pictures such as the following and keeping them in a file:

- Magazine pictures of people engaged in a hobby you want to begin.
- Snapshots of you and your family or friends having fun together.
- Pictures of the results of something you want to find time to do, such as a gourmet meal you want to try cooking or a hand-crafted oak desk if you want to try woodworking.
- An advertisement for the condo you want to purchase.
- Cartoons that depict your special situation.
- A travel flyer advertising a vacation spot you want to visit.
- A picture of the scene you want to view outside your office window (my picture is of the ocean)!
- A dollar bill with a larger figure written on it representing the amount you want in your savings account!

Periodically sit down with your file to remind yourself of what success looks like to you. It will keep you focused on your future. I guarantee it!

TAKING ACTION

I once heard a speaker say that only 2 percent of all Americans have the discipline to achieve their dreams. Of those who do not achieve their dreams, 23 percent do not know what they want and another 67 percent know, but do not know how to make it happen. The remaining 10 percent know what and how but lack discipline to follow through. In which category will you be?

Exhibit 11.2 provides you with an outline to begin to put your plans on paper. Why not start today?

💾 Exhibit 11.2. Action Plan.

Instructions: As you complete each step, check the box. The numbers in parentheses refer to exhibits in this book.

1. Do you know enough about the consulting profession?
   - ❑ Interview consultants that you know. (1.1)
   - ❑ Read about consulting. Scan the reading list at the end of the book.
   - ❑ Compare your values to the requirements of consulting.

2. Are you a match for the profession?
   - ❑ Compare your skills and characteristics to those required of a consultant. (2.1)
   - ❑ Measure your propensity as an entrepreneur. (2.2)

3. Do you know enough about consultant billing practices?
   - ❑ Calculate your financial requirements. (3.1)
   - ❑ Read about consulting billing structures.

4. Are you ready to start?
   - ❑ Describe your business, its services, and products.
   - ❑ Identify your market.
   - ❑ Analyze your competition.
   - ❑ Assess your skills.
   - ❑ Name your business.
   - ❑ Determine your pricing structure. (3.2, 3.3)
   - ❑ Identify start-up costs. (4.1)
   - ❑ Select an accountant.
   - ❑ Determine your business structure.
   - ❑ Check on zoning laws, licenses, taxes.
   - ❑ Select a location.
   - ❑ Develop a business plan that includes:
     - ❑ business description
     - ❑ marketing plan (5.1)
     - ❑ management plan
     - ❑ financial plan (4.2, 4.3, 4.4)
   - ❑ Select a banker, attorney, and insurance agent.
   - ❑ Arrange for financing or set aside capital for a worst-case scenario. (4.5)
   - ❑ File documentation to register your business legally.

💾 Exhibit 11.2. Action Plan, Cont'd.

5. Are you consistently marketing your services?
   - ❑ Complete and follow your marketing calendar. (5.2)
   - ❑ Identify potential client organizations and research them. (5.3)
   - ❑ Introduce your services with letters and telephone calls. (5.4)
   - ❑ Call on organizations in person. (5.5)
   - ❑ Maintain a client contact log. (5.6)

6. Do you have a handle on your expenses?
   - ❑ Maintain a monthly expense record. (6.1)
   - ❑ Track petty cash and expenditures. (6.2, 6.3)
   - ❑ Monitor invoices. (6.4)
   - ❑ Project revenue. (6.6)
   - ❑ Invoice clients in a timely manner. (6.5)
   - ❑ Track time and cost of specific projects. (6.7)
   - ❑ Compare project profits. (6.8)

7. Are you building professional client relationships?
   - ❑ Clarify expectations during the contracting phase with each client. (7.1)
   - ❑ Continue to build a partnership with each client. (7.2)

8. Are you ready to grow?
   - ❑ Explore various ways to build your business. (8.1, 8.2)
   - ❑ Ensure that expectations are clear when using subcontractors. (8.3, 8.4)

9. Do you consistently practice the highest ethical standards?

10. Are you professional in every respect?
    - ❑ Improve your skills.
    - ❑ Balance your life and your business.
    - ❑ Manage your time wisely. (10.1, 10.2, 10.3)
    - ❑ Mentor others.

11. Do you enjoy the profession as much as you thought you would?

GETTING READY

Perhaps you have read this far in this book. You're interested, but you are not quite ready. Perhaps you think you need a little more experience. Perhaps your financial situation is not stable enough to take the risk. Perhaps you are satisfied with the job you now have. But someday. . . .

What can you do? Don't lose the spark. Turn to Exhibit 11.3 and list fifty things you can do to move closer to becoming a consultant. List everything that comes to mind as fast as you can, such as read another book, join a professional organization, interview a consultant, take a course, attend a conference, invent a name for your consulting practice, identify a client with whom you would choose to work. All suggestions are good. Don't pause to judge or prioritize them now. Just write. Ready, set, go!

What can you do with your fifty ideas? It would seem natural for you to begin to put a plan together for how to go from here to there. It takes as much energy to wish as it does to plan. So go ahead. Wish on paper and make it become a plan.

Wish on paper and make it become a plan.

Instructions: List fifty things you can do to move closer to becoming a consultant.

1.	26.
2.	27.
3.	28.
4.	29.
5.	30.
6.	31.
7.	32.
8.	33.
9.	34.
10.	35.
11.	36.
12.	37.
13.	38.
14.	39.
15.	40.
16.	41.
17.	42.
18.	43.
19.	44.
20.	45.
21.	46.
22.	47.
23.	48.
24.	49.
25.	50.

READING LIST

Allerton, H. (1996, June). What things cost. *Training and Development.*

Baily, D., & Sproston, C. (1993). *Choosing and using training consultants.* Brookfield, VT: Gower, 20–23.

Bell, C. R., & Nadler, L. (1979). *The client-consultant handbook.* Houston, TX: Gulf.

Bellman, G. M. (1990). *The consultant's calling.* San Francisco, CA: Jossey-Bass.

Bellman, G. M., Block, P., & Boehm, B. (1986). Find the right consultant. *Info-Line,* 8610. Alexandria, VA: ASTD.

Biech, E. (1995, Summer). Ten mistakes CEOs make about training. *William & Mary Business Review,* 13–16.

Block, P. (1981). *Flawless consulting.* San Francisco, CA: Jossey-Bass/Pfeiffer.

Bond, W. J. (1997). *Going solo.* New York: McGraw-Hill.

Bourgeois, T., Goodhead, G., & Cooper, W. (1997). *The global management consulting marketplace: Key data, forecasts and trends.* Fitzwilliam, NH: Kennedy Information.

Cannon, J. T. (1990). *No miracles for hire.* New York: AMACOM.

Cohen, W. A. (1985). *How to make it big as a consultant.* New York: AMACOM.

Connor, R. A., Jr., & Davidson, J. P. (1985). *Marketing your consultant and professional services.* New York: John Wiley.

Consultant news. Fitzwilliam, NH: Kennedy Information.

Gacki, N. (1994, May). Becoming an organizational development consultant. *ODN Newsletter.*

Gendelman, J. (1995). *Consulting 101.* Alexandria, VA: ASTD.

Gilley, J. W., & Coffern, A. J. (1994). *Internal consulting for HRD professionals.* Alexandria, VA: ASTD.

Goodman, G. S. (1997). *Six-figure consulting.* New York: AMACOM.

Greenbaum, T. L. (1990). *The consultant's manual.* New York: John Wiley.

Holtz, H. (1993). *How to succeed as an independent consultant.* New York: John Wiley.

Holtz, H. (1994). *The business plan guide for independent consultants.* New York: John Wiley.

Kennedy Information. (1997). *The global management consulting marketplace: Key data forecasts and trends.* Fitzwilliam, NH: Author.

Kintler, D., & Adams, B. (1998). *Streetwise independent consulting.* Holbrook, MA: Adams Media.

Lewin, M. D. (1995). *The overnight consultant.* New York: John Wiley.

Lewin, M. D. (1997). *The consultant's survival guide.* New York: John Wiley.

Peters, T. (1997). The brand called you. *Fast Magazine,* Aug.-Sept., 83–94.

Schiffman, S. (1988). *The consultant's handbook.* Holbrook, MA: Adams Media.

Shefsky, L. E. (1994). *Entrepreneurs are made, not born.* New York: McGraw-Hill.

Shenson, H. L. (1990). *How to select and manage consultants.* San Francisco, CA: Jossey-Bass/Pfeiffer.

Stein, C. (1994, November 15). Millions for their thoughts: Management consulting finds big, profitable place in cutthroat economy. *Boston Globe.*

Sujansky, J. G. (1991). *The power of partnering.* San Francisco, CA: Jossey-Bass/Pfeiffer.

Tepper, R. (1993). *The consultant's proposal, fee, and contract problem-solver.* New York: John Wiley.

Tepper, R. (1995). *The 10 hottest consulting practices.* New York: John Wiley.

Tuller, L. W. (1992). *The independent consultant's Q & A book.* Holbrook, MA: Adams Media.

Viney, N. (1994). *Bluff your way in consulting.* Nashville, TN: Associated Publishers Group and Ravette Books.

Weinberg, G. M. (1985). *The secrets of consulting.* New York: Dorset House.

Weiss, A. (1992). *Million dollar consulting.* New York: McGraw-Hill.

Elaine Biech is president and managing principal of ebb associates, with offices in Portage, Wisconsin, and Norfolk, Virginia. The human resource development firm specializes in the custom design of training programs and consulting services. Biech has been in the consulting field for seventeen years and has developed training packages for health-care institutions; the insurance, banking, and shipbuilding industries; manufacturing businesses; and government and nonprofit organizations.

She has developed media presentations and training manuals and has presented at dozens of regional and national conferences. She is well known for custom-designed projects for management, supervision, training, and communication topics. She is known as a trainers' trainer.

As a management consultant, trainer, and designer, Biech has provided services to Land O'Lakes, McDonald's, Lands' End, General Casualty Insurance, CUNA Mutual Insurance Group, American Family Insurance, Hershey Chocolate, Johnson Wax, the Federal Reserve Bank, the U.S. Navy, NASA, Coopers & Lybrand, ASTD, the American Red Cross, the State of Wisconsin, the State of Minnesota, the University of Wisconsin, and numerous other public- and private-sector organizations.

Biech specializes in helping people work in teams to maximize their effectiveness. She implements corporate-wide systems such as quality improvement, reengineering of business processes, and mentoring programs and facilitates topics such as assertiveness, coaching today's employees, fostering creativity, customer relations, time management, stress management, speaking skills, training competence, conducting productive meetings, managing change, handling difficult employees, organizational communication, conflict resolution, and effective listening.

Biech has co-authored more than a dozen books and articles, including *The ASTD Source Book: Creativity and Innovation—Widen Your Spectrum* (McGraw-Hill & ASTD, 1996); "Ten Mistakes CEOs Make About Training," in *William & Mary Business Review,* Summer 1995; and "So You Want to Be a Consultant," in *Careers and the MBA,* Winter 1994.

She received her B.S. degree in business and education consulting and her master's degree in Human Resource Development from the University of Wisconsin-Superior. Biech is a member of the American Society for Training and Development (ASTD), American Society for Quality Control (ASQC), Association for Quality and Participation (AQP), Organization Development Network (ODN), and the National Professional Speakers' Association (NSA). Biech is the recipient of the 1992 National Torch Award from ASTD. She was also selected as the 1995 Wisconsin Women Entrepreneurs' Ann Randall Mentor Award winner.

Cost-effectiveness, of hiring consultants, 4, 5

Costs. *See* Expenses

Courier services, 69

Creativity: accountant with, 56–57; for gaining experience, 73; in mailings, 86–87, 90; in marketing, 89–95; as reason for becoming consultant, 7

Credit, line of, 26, 125

Credit cards, business, 126

D

Daily rates: charging by, 44–45, 47; myth about, 7–9; range of, 38–39; for subcontractors, 191; value given client related to, 136

Days: billable, 40–41, 44–45; defining, 47; rate for half, 47

Details, attention to, 16, 17

Double dipping, 192

Dues: affordability of, 199; tracking expenses for, 129, 131

E

E-mail, 129, 133, 225

Edison, T., 197

Einstein, A., 1

Employees: consultants as, 3; hiring, for growth, 166–168, 169; temporary, 4, 180

Entertainment, tracking expenses for, 129, 131

Entrepreneurs: personal characteristics of, 29–32; work hours of, 10, 15–16

Equipment: leasing versus purchasing, 126; maintenance of, 143, 146; tracking expenses for, 129, 131, 132

Ethics, 187–195; in charging clients, 187, 191–192; in client's actions, 194–195; code of, 195; in consultant's actions, 187–192; in delivery of services, 188–191; of pricing, 50–52, 191; reputation and, 188, 195; in subcontracting, 192–193

Expenses, 121; actual, and budget, 128, 142; avoiding, for marketing plan development,

81–83; ethical considerations with, 192; invoiced directly to clients, 125; out-of-pocket, project initiation fees to cover, 124–125; reimbursable, 48–49, 140; start-up, 26, 61, 64–66; subcontractor, 177; time invested versus value received and, 143; tracking, 128–133, 134, 177. *See also specific expenses*

Experience: depth and breadth of, 22–23; gaining, 71–73

Expertise: of consultants, 4, 10; as defining niche, 66

F

Family, support from, 28

Faxes: cover page for, 69, 70; tracking expenses for, 129, 133

Federal employer-identification number (FEIN), 57

Fees: conditional, 46; increasing, 49–50, 52; methods of calculating, 40–43; myth about, 7–9; percentage, 46–47; pricing strategy for, 43–44; pricing structures for, 44–47, 50–51, 191; project initiation, 124–125; range of, 38–39; reducing, 51–52; reimbursable charges included in, 48–49; for subcontractors, 51, 129, 132, 181, 191; value given clients related to, 50, 136. *See also* Pricing

Filing system, 210, 218–219, 223

Financial planning, 60–64, 65, 122

Financial statement, personal, 65

Flawless Consulting (Block), 106, 152, 205

Ford, H., 19

Forms. *See* Sample documents/forms

Freedom: as reason for becoming consultant, 5, 6, 7; to set schedules, 222

Furniture, tracking expenses for, 129, 131

G

Gendelman, J., 208

Gifts, promotional, 84

Giving back, 48, 73, 199, 216, 223–224

Global Management Consulting Marketplace, The (Kennedy Information), 1

Goals, in marketing plan, 79–80

Government agencies: fees for consulting in, 39; marketing to, 93; payment on contracts with, 124; per diem travel rate for, 48–49; pricing structure with, 45

Graduate students, as interns, 178–179

Growth, 165–186; becoming subcontractor for, 180–181; collaboration for, 182–183; of consulting profession, 1, 3–7; current business practices and, 185–186; hiring interns for, 178–179; hiring staff for, 166–168, 169; hiring subcontractors for, 173–178; joint ventures for, 181–182; monitoring, 143, 144–145; myth about, 11–12; offering additional services for, 183–184; partnerships for, 165–166, 168, 170–173; practice structure for, 173; product production for, 184–185; selecting method for, 165, 186; using temporary service for, 180

Guarantee, of satisfaction with services, 53–54, 92

H

Handshake, 150

Health, of entrepreneurs, 30

Home offices, 222–223; advantages of, 27, 65–66, 209; disadvantages of, 13, 27; telephone lines for, 69

Hourly rate, charging by, 45

I

Image. *See* Professional image

Income: determining required, 35–38; lack of steady, 26. *See also* Salaries

Independence: creating client's, 157, 190; as reason for becoming consultant, 5, 6, 7

Independent consultants, as way to enter field, 3, 29

Independent contractors, 178–179

Institute of Management Consultants, 195, 199

Instructional Systems Association, 199

Insurance, tracking expenses for, 129, 131

Interest, tracking expenses for, 129, 132

Internal Revenue Service, independent contractor guidelines of, 178–179. *See also* Taxes

Interns, hiring, 178–179

Invoices, 121; delivery system for, 123–124; format for, 69, 137, 139; late payment/nonpayment on, 126–127, 140; paying, 127–128; prepayment/early payment discount on, 125; for repeat billings to client, 210; small business mentioned on, 126; tracking, 137, 138

Isolation, 27, 170

J

Jefferson, T., 187

Joint Travel Regulations, 49

Joint ventures: for growth, 181–182; versus collaboration, 182

Junk mail, 86, 205

K

Keller, H., 217

Kennedy Information, 1, 3

L

Land O'Lakes, 163

Learning. *See* Professional development

Leasing equipment, 126

Legal fees, tracking expenses for, 129, 130

Letters: reflecting professional image, 68; sample introductory marketing, 98–103

Liability, business structure and, 57, 58

Licenses, tracking expenses for, 129, 132

Life, balancing business and, 207–209

Limitations, personal, 17

Limited liability companies (LLCs), 58

Line of credit, 26, 125

Listening, 149, 162

Loans: line of credit for, 26, 125; tracking interest paid on, 129, 132

51–52; as skill of consultants, 22; strategy for, 43–44; structures for, 44–47, 50–51, 191; talking to clients about, 52–53. *See also* Fees

Printing, tracking expenses for, 129, 131

Pro bono work, 48, 73, 224. *See also* Volunteer work

Product production, for growth, 184–185

Professional development: finding time for, 219, 224; strategies for, 202, 204–207; tracking expenses for, 129, 132

Professional fees, 129, 132, 181, 191

Professional image, 68–71; in initial meeting with client, 150; as measure of success, 75–76

Professional journals, 129, 131, 205

Professional organizations: membership in, 199, 205; tracking dues to, 129, 131; volunteer work for, 199, 216

Professionalism, 197–216; competencies of, 198–202, 203; giving back for, 216; image and, 71; life/business balance and, 207–209; professional development for, 202, 204–207; time management and, 209–216

Profit: cash flow and, 122–123; monitoring, 142–143, 144–145; versus salary, 41

Projects: client-consultant relationship after, 163–164; fixed-price, 45–46; increased size of, 3–4; initiation fees for, 124–125; monitoring profitability of, 143, 144–145; turning down, 17, 118, 189

Proposals, 107–108; charging for, 48; project initiation fees in, 124–125; sample, 109–113

Prospecting, as consultant skill, 20

Purchasing equipment, 126

Q

Questions: to ask potential clients, 104; asked by clients, 106; for building relationship with client, 154; for interviewing consultants, 14

R

Record keeping: accountant tickler file, 210; colored folders, 210, 218–219, 223; tracking expenses, 128–133, 134, 177

Referrals: from clients, 88, 148, 160; to other consultants, 90

Refusing assignments, 17, 118, 189

Relationships: building, 150–159, 202; marketing through, 87–88. *See also* Client-consultant relationship

Rent, tracking expense for, 129, 132

Repairs, tracking expenses for, 129, 132

Repeat business, 88, 148

Reputation: client's payment, 124; constant building of, 10; of consulting profession, 11, 16; ethics and, 188, 195

Request for Proposals (RFP), 45, 93

Resources: in marketing plan, 80; professional development, 205; tracking expenses for, 129, 133

Retainers, 46

Revenues, projecting, 140, 141

Routine, avoiding, 6

S

S corporations, 58, 168

Salaries, 3, 7–9; determining, 36, 37; of employees of consulting firms, 3; of partners, 170; tracking expenses for, 129, 133; versus profit, 41

Sales meetings, charging for, 48

Sample documents/forms: actions to become consultant, 230–231, 233; assessing professional competencies, 203; building relationship with client, 153, 158–159; calculating required income, 37; considering hiring staff, 169; contract, 114–117; determining partner compatibility, 171–172; determining what to charge clients, 37, 41, 42; fax cover page, 70; financial planning, 61–64, 65; hiring subcontractors, 174–177; invoicing, 138–139; loaning out books, 146; marketing plan, 78, 82; marketing to potential clients, 97–103, 105; monitoring project profitability, 144–145; petty cash, 135; projecting revenue, 141; proposal, 109–113; time management, 213–215; tracking expenses, 129, 134; visualizing success, 227–228

Saying "no," 17, 118, 189

Schedule, 222, 226; free time, 10, 208, 221–222; work hours, 10, 15–16, 221–222

Secrets of Consulting, The (Weinberg), 75

Security, 6, 16

Self-discipline, required for consulting, 17

Self-employment, as way to enter field, 3, 29

Selling yourself, skill in, 17, 20

Seminar expenses, tracking, 129, 133

Services: elements of, 156; ethical delivery of, 188–191; guaranteeing, 53–54, 92; offering additional, 183–184

Shefsky, L. E., 16

Sherman Anti-Trust Act, 43

Skills: communication, 16–17, 18, 200; for initial meeting with clients, 149–150; needed for consulting, 15–18, 20–23, 24, 199–200

Small businesses: invoice mention of, 126; marketing to, 84–85; pension plans for, 132

Small claims court, for bad debts, 140

Social Security number, 57

Sole proprietorships, 57

Specialization, 22, 23

Staff. *See* Employees

Start-up, 55–74; checklist for, 74; costs of, 26, 61, 64–66; determining your niche, 66–67; ease of, 6, 11; landing first clients, 71–73; marketing time during, 11, 88; networking during, 72–73; personal considerations before, 26–28; planning for, 71–72; preparing business plan, 59–64, 65; presenting professional image, 68–71; selecting accountant for, 13, 56–57; selecting business structure for, 57–59

Stationery, 68, 69, 91

Stein, C., 4

Stone, W. C., 187

Subcontractors: agreement with, 174–176; becoming, 3, 51, 73, 180–181; competition from, 178, 193; ethics with, 192–193; expense record for, 177; fees for, 51, 181, 191; to grow business, 173–178, 180–181; hiring, 173–178; as independent contractors, 178

Subscriptions, tracking expenses for, 129, 131

Success: measures of, 75–76; visualizing, 226–229

Support: backup business, 27; family, 28

T

Tasks: fees based on, 48; pricing structures for, 51

Taxes: business structure and, 57–58; expense tracking and, 130; providing for, 8, 36; with subcontractors, 178; tracking, 129, 133

Technology, as reason for becoming consultant, 6

Telephone: business line, 69; time management for, 210; tracking expenses for, 129, 133

Temporary services, hiring employees from, 180

3× Rule, 36

Tickler file, 210, 229

Time: for bill paying, 127–128; for billing, 123; constraints on, as favoring consultants, 4–5; expenses and, 143; free, 10, 208, 221–222; for marketing, 11, 83, 88; as service delivery element, 156; travel, charging for, 49; work, 10, 15–16, 221–222

Time management, 209–216; in business procedures, 209–210; during travel, 210–211; forms for, 212–216; tips for, 211–212

Training: conducting, 22; with other consultants, 206; per person pricing structure for, 46

Travel: amount of, 222–223, 225; ethical considerations with, 192; expenses for, 48–49, 94, 129, 133, 134, 140, 177; per diem rate for, 48–49, 187; as reason for becoming consultant, 7; simplification for, 219, 224–225; with small consulting firms, 28; time management during, 210–211

Turning down work, 17, 118, 189

2× Rule, 36

U

Unemployment, as reason for becoming consultant, 6

Utilities, tracking expenses for, 129, 133

V

Value: expenses/time invested and, 143; fees related to, 50, 136; given client, 164

Virtual partnerships, for growth, 181–182

Visualization, 226–229

Volunteer work, 199, 216, 223–224. *See also* Pro bono work

W

Website, creating, 92

Weinberg, G. M., 75, 88

Weiss, A., 46

Wilde, O., 35

Work: informing client of, 136; location's effect on, 222; niche defined by, 66; part-time, 3, 71–72; pro bono, 48, 73, 224; turning down, 17, 118, 177; volunteer, 199, 216, 223–224

World Wide Web, 205

Writing: books, 184, 221; for marketing, 91; skills in, 16–17

Get the classic guides no practitioner can do without!

A how-to guide for consultants

Gordon Lippitt & Ronald Lippitt

THE CONSULTING PROCESS IN ACTION
Second Edition

Here is the accumulation of 35 years of work of two men who have helped shape the training and development field. Teachers, trainers, consultants, and continual learners themselves, the authors share their repertoire of concepts, strategies, and techniques.

Learn to:

- ■ **Recognize** the phases in consulting
- ■ **Cope** with ethical dilemmas
- ■ **Assess** and evaluate your projects
- ■ **Consult** in international settings
- ■ **Facilitate** change . . . and much more!

The authors identify the six phases of almost any consultant–client working relationship: • engaging in initial contact and entry • formulating a contract and establishing a helping relationship • identifying problems through diagnostic analysis • setting goals and planning for action • taking action and cycling feedback • completing the contract.

> *"The function of consultants is part of the role and function of all those who lead, direct, teach, or interact as friends and peers with others."—Gordon and Ronald Lippitt, authors*

This book emphasizes the role of the consultant—internal or external—in an organizational setting. You'll learn to recognize the most appropriate, effective, and credible route to solving almost any consulting conundrum. You'll use every chart, checklist, and reference in this work to improve your own job performance.

You might call yourself a "consultant." You might not. Regardless, you'll find yourself better equipped for any business interaction when you have this book at your side.

paperback / 213 pages

The Consulting Process in Action / **Code D762** / **$29.95**

A consultant's bible

Peter Block

FLAWLESS CONSULTING
A Guide to Getting Your Expertise Used

Focus on what makes for successful consulting with this practical, how-to-do-it guidebook. This run-away best-seller applies to anyone who does consulting, even if you don't call yourself a consultant. Author Peter Block describes it this way: "You are consulting any time you are trying to change or improve a situation but have no direct control over the implementation."

Flawless Consulting delves into the science of effective consulting . . . whether one works on a formal client basis, or one works as an employee within a multilayered company. Through the use of illustrative examples, case studies, and exercises, Block details the behaviors behind interpersonal dynamics and error-free consulting.

Using the techniques in this book, you will learn how to:

- ■ **Encourage** the demand for your expertise
- ■ **Ensure** that your recommendations are implemented more frequently
- ■ **Develop** a partnership role with clients
- ■ **Avoid** no-win consulting situations
- ■ **Increase** the leverage you have with your clients
- ■ **Establish** more trusting relationships with clients . . . and much more!

Flawless Consulting, a best-seller for the ages, points out the elements that often get in the way of productive consulting. Then it shows you how to hurdle these barriers and how to progress to clear, mutually-beneficial consulting.

Based on the author's extensive internal and external consulting experience, this book will serve as an in-depth guide for developing the necessary skills for getting your expertise used, even when you don't have control. Thousands and thousands of professionals swear by this unmistakable, irreplacable guide—and you will too!

hardcover / 214 pages

Flawless Consulting / **Code A897** / **$39.95**

The Consultant's Duo / **Code F886** / includes one copy each of The Consulting Process in Action and Flawless Consulting / **$59.95**

CALL FREE: 800.274.4434   FAX FREE: 800.569.0443

EXHIBITS ON DISK

The minimum configuration needed to utilize the files included on this disk is a computer system with one 3.5" floppy disk drive capable of reading double-sided high-density IBM formatted floppy disks and word processing or desktop publishing software able to read Microsoft WORD 6.0/95 files. Document memory needs will vary, but your system should be capable of opening file sizes of 50+K. No monitor requirements other than the ones established by your document software need be met.

Each of the exhibits in your textbook that are marked with a disk icon have been saved onto the enclosed disk as a Microsoft WORD 6.0/95 file. These files can be opened with many Windows- and Macintosh-based word processors or desktop publishers for viewing or editing as you see fit. The files were originally created and saved as a WORD 6.0/95 DOC file by Microsoft Word 97. Not all software will read the files exactly the same, but the DOC format is an honest attempt by Jossey-Bass/Pfeiffer Publishers to preserve the composition of the exhibits such as borders, fonts, character attributes, bullets, and so on as accurately as possible.

Copy all DOC files to a directory/folder in your computer system. To read the files using your Windows-based document software, select File from the main menu followed by Open to display the Open dialog box. Set the correct drive letter and subdirectory shown in the Open dialog box by using the Look in control. In the Files of type text box enter *.doc to display the list of DOC files available in the subdirectory.

Each file name is coded to its exhibit in the text to make it easy for you to find the one you want. For example, the Exhibit 5.4a is named EXH05-4A.DOC. You can open the file by either double-clicking your mouse on the file name that you want to open or by clicking once on the file name to select it and then once on the Open command button.